ASTONISHING

Experience God's Immeasurable Father-Love for You

LOVE

John G. Hutchinson

ASTOUNDING LOVE: EXPERIENCE GOD'S IMMEASURABLE
FATHER-LOVE FOR YOU

ISBN: 978-1-77069-141-4

Printed in Canada.

Word Alive Press
131 Cordite Road, Winnipeg, MB R3W 1S1
www.wordalivepress.ca

Library and Archives Canada Cataloguing in Publication

Hutchinson, John G., 1932–
    Astounding love : experience God's immeasurable father–love for you
/ John G. Hutchinson.

ISBN 978-1-77069-141-4

    1. God (Christianity)--Love. 2. Love--Religious aspects--Christianity.
I. Title.

BT140.H87 2010   231.6   C2010-907223-5

Endorsements for *Astounding Love*

I am honored to endorse this book. In the years that I have known John Hutchinson, two things have stood out to me: his love for God and his commitment to prayer. But John's new book, *Astounding Love*, is not, first and foremost, about his love for God. Rather it is an intimate and tender account of God's great love for John—and for us all.

If this sounds a bit too 'saccharine' for your taste, no need to worry. John is not only a lover; he is also a teacher, and in this book he offers one of the most thorough and systematic rationales for intimacy with God. Men, especially, will like this. So do yourself a favor and spend some time with this wonderful primer. It is bound to refresh the most important relationship you will ever have!

George Otis Jr.
Founder and Executive Director of The Sentinel Group
Producer of the Transformation Videos

It is an honor to write an endorsement for *Astounding Love*. This is no ordinary book, since it has been born out of many years of ministry and is full of proven principles.

It is a living story of love and trust between God Himself and a redeemed sinner named John Hutchinson who has chosen to walk the way of the Cross, irrespective of the cost. This is a love built upon intimacy, revelation, perseverance, discipline, and a deep desire to know the ways of the Lord. For many decades, John has poured himself into knowing the Word of God. He has prayed and wept for God's end–time "outpouring of the Holy Spirit" for himself and for Christ's whole church. You will quickly see how God has responded with profound love and revelation.

If you are serious about wanting transformation in your own life, this book is for you. It will radically challenge your walk with God and will powerfully impact your understanding of ministry.

John is a treasure to the Body of Christ, and this book will clearly cause the reader to search for that deeper understanding of "*Christ, in whom are hidden all the treasures of wisdom and knowledge*" (Colossians 2:2–3).

Rev. Dr. Alistair P. Petrie
Founder and Executive Director of
Partnership Ministries

I'm convinced that the root of most relational conflicts and inner bondage is a lack of revelation of the Father–heart of God. Truly knowing and experiencing the love of God is the only path to freedom and wholeness. John's book, *Astounding Love*, takes readers from mere head knowledge to transformative heart revelation. People who read this book will not just *know* God's love—they will *experience* God's love in a way that will revolutionize their relationship with God and with people.

The Bible says that anyone who truly comprehends the magnitude of God's love will be filled with His fullness (Ephesians

3:18–19). *Astounding Love* will immerse you so deeply in God's love that you will never be the same. It will release you from fear, insecurity, and other hindrances that have stood in the way of you becoming the person God created you to be. The end result? You will be propelled into the incredible destiny God has planned for your life. If you only have time to read one book this year, I urge you to read *Astounding Love*. It's not just a book—it is a profound and liberating experience with God that will transform you from the inside out!

Judy Rushfeldt
Award–winning author, speaker,
and online magazine publisher

If you desire to know God personally, as the Scriptures declare we can, and if you want to avoid the false ideas about God that we find in this satanically–deceived world, this book is an excellent resource.

If the goal of our salvation is to really experience God, there are two indispensible things we need to pursue. First, we need to know the revealed facts about God, as our foundation. Second, we need to know God personally and intimately.

John has captured both of these aspects as he leads the reader into knowing and experiencing the Father–heart of God. He illuminates the truth about the Father in a way which draws the human heart into humility, and into a desire for deeper intimacy with Him. It did for me!

Allen G. Fode
Director of Ellel Ministries of Western Canada

A few years back, I invited John to speak about the Father–heart of God to a group of university students and young professionals. Two things impacted me that weekend. One was the passion and wisdom that John spoke with as he shared his journey of intimacy with his heavenly Father. The other was the level of hunger and fervor of the young people as they were soaking it in! *Astounding Love* contains the same passion and wisdom that was so impacting that weekend. New life will be breathed into your relationship with your heavenly Dad. John's unwavering use of Scripture, along with his personal stories of his own walk with God, will deepen your intimacy with God. This book speaks across generational lines to the core need of a largely fatherless generation.

Michael Jones
Lead Pastor of The Living Room Church,
Montreal, Québec

The first verse of a great hymn begins by saying: "The Love of God is greater far than tongue or pen can ever tell…" This is so true! John has touched on one side of God's great heart that is often forgotten, overlooked, misconstrued, or sadly neglected.

Astounding Love is not a particularly easy or casual read. John deeply desires to draw the reader into an intimate encounter with the True and Living God, and to personally experience His wonderful Father–heart of love. It is John's emphasis on the importance of the Word of God, and his use of many Scriptures, that gives the passion and the power to this book. It is great for personal study, but also a wonderful text for small group studies.

I trust and pray that the Holy Spirit will mightily use this work of faith and labor of love to draw many closer to the Lord Jesus Christ, and into the loving arms of God our Heavenly Father. "Let's Ask Him!"

Rev. Don Harbridge
Formerly: Western Canada Representative
for Word Publishing, Inc.

John Hutchinson and I have served Christ in a close relationship for many years, in India and in Canada, in youth evangelism and disciple training. I am pleased and delighted to unreservedly endorse this most powerful and articulate teaching of God's true love, as revealed to him through the Bible and the Holy Spirit.

There is a great need for the twenty–first century followers of Jesus Christ to clearly understand and experience the true essence and nature of God's immense love for all people. This book will surely help to fill that need.

John's lifelong study, praying, and seeking the wisdom of the Holy Spirit has produced this highly valuable book for both believers and truth–seekers. You will not be disappointed.

It is like finding the ultimate diamond amidst a lot of "everything but the real thing."

Rev. John L. Teibe
Formerly: Director of Southeast Asia Youth For Christ
Formerly: Director of Youth For Christ Canada

Writing with the grace of a teacher's gifting, Grandpa John (as he is affectionately known to many of us young people) teaches who God is and reveals the grandeur of God's heart towards His children. Understanding the Father–heart of God is one of the most important teachings this generation needs to embrace. Let these spiritual truths go deep into the core of your being. As you read this book, you will discover that God's love for you is, indeed, astounding!

Dwight Van Middlesworth, Jr.
University Student

DEDICATION

First of all, I dedicate this book to:
 our great, loving Heavenly Father and
  His beloved Son, Jesus Christ, our Savior.
   May They give, by the precious Holy Spirit,
    to many people, both young and old, rich and poor,
     a deep experience of the astounding, immeasurable,
      Father–Love of God, for His whole human race!

Secondly, I lovingly dedicate this book to:
 Reta, my dear wife, who was a wonderful,
  loving, faithful, supportive, and vivacious partner
   in both our marriage and in our service to Jesus Christ.
    God graciously gave us a good and eventful marriage
     for over fifty–three years, both in Canada and in India.
      God used her to uniquely bless many, many people!

And then God took her Home;
 now she is doing what she loved most:
  singing, praising, and dancing around His throne.
   As someone said at her Going–Home Party,
    "She will also be making all the angels laugh."
     Reta—a zest for life and a great sense of humor!

Thanks, Reta, for your many loving encouragements and exhortations to finish this book!

Acknowledgements

I sincerely and wholeheartedly thank the many fellow believers who urged me to write this book.

I thank you, Theora Meyers, for all your initial transcribing and typing. It got me started!

Thanks also to the many who kept on asking me, "How's the book coming along?" And this certainly includes my wife, Reta. You all kept me going! Without you I likely wouldn't have persevered so long!

Much gratitude also goes to a dear friend, Janice Pasay, who has helped me very, very much. She was one of my students when I taught these truths in Bible school. Recently, she volunteered to assist me in getting the manuscript finished and ready for publishing. She did a great amount of research on authoring, editing, and publishing. She has also done a lot of typing, editing, and advising me. Her help has been most valuable!

I am deeply grateful to my family members, friends, and colleagues who have taken the time and effort to peruse and critique my very rough draft manuscript. They have given me much good advice and many needed and helpful suggestions, as well as encouragement. Thank you very much! God bless you all!

TABLE OF CONTENTS

Part Three: The Wonderful Father–Heart of God

INTRODUCTION

A STUNNING GLIMPSE INTO THE HEART OF GOD—IN A MOVIE THEATER

God has a great sense of humor! This amazing insight into the wonderful, loving 'Heart' of God began for me in a movie theater. It's humorous because I was brought up in a strict family that believed we should not go to movie theaters. But after God filled my wife and me with His Holy Spirit in a much greater measure, He began to liberate us from these manmade, religious rules. So at the urging of some friends, we went to see the movie *Fiddler on the Roof*, which they had so highly recommended.

Now, no doubt it is a good movie, full of mankind's great joys and great sorrows, human loveliness and human ugliness. But near the end of the movie, something happened to me that was far beyond anything the movie itself could have ever done. I received a wonderful visitation from God. It was a very deep and overwhelming realization, a revelation, of two realities which were far beyond anything that I could have imagined on my own.

HEAVEN ON EARTH

First, God showed me what He originally intended for all of us humans to experience and enjoy on earth. It is still far beyond my power to adequately describe the greatness and beauty of

the complete love, relationship, harmony,
unity, peace, contentment, happiness, joy,
delight, pleasure, enjoyment, fulfillment,
goodness, kindness, tenderness, health,
purpose, destiny, and righteousness

that God wanted and planned for us, His earthly children, to enjoy, along with Him as our Father.

This astounding revelation opened my eyes to the wonderful and indescribable love and goodness of God's Heart for every one of us humans whom He created, and whom He loves so intensely. This revelation greatly transformed and deepened my personal love for God—and it still continues to do so. This was a side of God I hardly knew at all. He is so utterly wonderful!

HELL ON EARTH

But then God imposed upon this superbly glorious reality something horribly opposite to it. God showed me the depth and ugly reality of what sin and satan have done to the human race, in stark contrast to the great love and goodness that God intended for us. It is also beyond my power to adequately describe

the pain, brokenness, suffering, sorrow,
agony, misery, enmity, anger, bitterness,
unforgiveness, malice, hatred, murder,
sickness, death, fear, anguish, rejection,
greed, poverty, brutality, abuse, and injustice

that God showed me.

Through this second revelation, God opened my eyes to the horrible vindictiveness, vicious hatred, murderous maliciousness, and vile destructiveness of satan's nature and character. This horrible second realization highlighted all the more, by extreme contrast, the glorious, true love and goodness of God's wonderful Heart towards us, which is a side of God so few people really know and experience.

These two totally opposite revelations, so vividly superimposed against each other, were almost more than I could bear. I was overwhelmed! I began to sob from the deepest part of my being. But being in a crowded theater, I had to sob silently. My wife couldn't imagine what was happening to me. We were the last to leave the theater, and I couldn't compose myself enough to tell her about it until we were more than halfway home.

Can you see what a delightful sense of humor God has? He gave me such an astonishing and beautiful revelation of His immeasurable love and goodness while watching a secular movie—in a movie theater, not in a church.

REVOLUTIONIZED RELATIONSHIPS

From then on, every time I would read through the Bible, I would increasingly see the wonderful goodness, love, mercy, grace, patience, forgiveness, and beauty of God, whereas before I was mostly blind to it. I also began to increasingly see the hateful and destructive nature of satan, and what he has done—and is still doing—to us, the precious children God so lovingly created. This profoundly ignited and revolutionized my love–relationship with God.

For when I was about sixteen years old, I heard a sermon

that painted a picture of God the Father as The Boss and The Judge, someone who was harsh and stern and was about to condemn and punish us sinners. According to the sermon, Jesus stepped in between us and The Boss, held Him off by dying for our sin on the cross, and rescued us from the wrath of The Judge. This left a lasting impression in my mind that God was the "bad guy" and Jesus was the "good guy." This picture is twisted and very wrong.

God's Scriptures are very clear that it was the Father's great love for us that sent Jesus, His Son, to come to the earth to live and to die for our sins, so that we could be forgiven, cleansed, and welcomed back into God's great, loving Father–Arms. This stunning revelation in the movie theater healed my twisted concept of God and revealed the beauty of the other side of God I hardly knew.

Many years later, when teaching in a Bible school, I incorporated this insight of God's wonderful Heart into one of my courses. To my amazement, I found that it was profoundly affecting many students (some even to tears), and was leading them into a new and closer love–relationship with God than they had ever imagined was possible.

I then developed this course material into a seminar, and found it to have the same effect on many people in many places. I was asked quite a few times to put this into a book, but I kept shrugging it off by saying, "I'm just not the book–type." But God eventually made it very clear to me that I was to write this book. This book is about the other side of God, the side that is so often missing in the hearts and minds of many people.

A Manmade God?

A lot of people think they know quite a bit about God and what He is really like. Others just have some vague ideas about Him. But almost all of us have a very limited understanding of His truly wonderful loving Heart of goodness. And I have found that many of us have some very wrong concepts of what He is *genuinely* like, deep inside His inner nature, the very core of His loving personality.

Many people try to construct their own image of God out of what they want, or out of what they think He ought to be. This manmade "fantasy god" of theirs is not real. God created us in His image—we cannot create Him in the image we want Him to be. He is the eternal, unchanging, sovereign, supreme God. And we are created by Him to be His dear children.

The Main Thing

The main thing I want to describe for you in this book, as completely as I can and with God's help, is the Scriptural truth and the Scriptural balance of our great Creator's amazing loving nature, disposition, temperament, and character—which is His beautiful goodness.

I will base this only on the Word of God, not on human perceptions, ideas, philosophies, or theologies. Nor will I base it on what I myself may think or presume.

WHAT GOD SAYS ABOUT HIMSELF

This will *not* be about what man says about God, but what God says about Himself in His own Word, the Bible: what His inner nature really *is*, and what His inner nature really *is not*.

This will *not* be all that there is to know about God, because we will be discovering more and more about Him for the rest of our lives—and likely for all of eternity, too. I will try to give you, as God enables me through His Scripture, as full and as balanced a picture as I can of the main aspects of His wonderful character, nature, temperament, and disposition—His good and perfect Father-Heart.

When I refer to God's Heart, I mean His innermost being, the very central part of His nature, the core of His character, and the vital essence of His temperament and personality.

God is so great, so glorious, so good, and so loving, that the highest of human vocabulary utterly fails to adequately describe Him. Therefore, in this book you will find superlative descriptions and ultimate kinds of words. Please believe me, I am *not* trying to hype God or sell Him to you. He is so truly wonderful that He does not need to be hyped. But the highest and greatest things I can say about God are still far short of all His true, immeasurable glory and goodness.

First, we will briefly explore the great and awesome external attributes of God our Creator. Then we will dive more fully into His beautiful inner character and nature (disposition, temperament, and personality). Finally, we will look at what an absolutely wonderful, passionately loving, and perfect Father He is to us.

I am following this sequence because the kind of person

God is determines what kind of a Father He is. For example, if a selfish, mean, stingy, harsh, unloving, cold, and cruel man becomes a father, he will continue to be that same way as a father. But if he is a loving, affectionate, caring, tender, patient, generous, and forgiving man, those attributes will define the kind of father he is. So first of all, we must find out the true nature and character of God. Then we will begin to see what kind of a wonderful Father this God will be to us.

EXPERIENCE HIM!

I want this to be simple and understandable, yet it will be deep and awe–inspiring as well. I hope it will be readable and thrilling to both young and old, and to Christians and non–Christians alike. My prayer is that you, the reader, will receive from God a great and authentic revelation, and that you will truly experience God's wonderful Father–Heart, which will revolutionize your life—and change your eternity.

The overall purpose of this book is for you to experience, for yourself, a true and uninhibited love/trust relationship with God, your Heavenly Father, through a Scripturally accurate, balanced, and ever–growing knowledge of His wonderful, truly loving Father–Heart.

At the end of each chapter, there is a short section entitled "Let's Ask Him"—like the one below. This may help you, but also feel very free to use your own words, from your own heart.

LET'S ASK HIM:

> God, I would like to know what You truly are like, deep inside Your Heart. I'm not sure what I'm going find, but I'd like to know.

> Please show me Who You are and what You are really like in Your inner nature.

> Help my spirit to recognize and receive the truth of Your Word.

> I would like to personally experience Your great, astounding love and goodness.

> God, I ask You this in Jesus' name.

PART ONE

Really Knowing God, Personally

CHAPTER ONE

THE MAN WHO THOUGHT HE KNEW GOD

And His Very Surprising Prayer

Of all the people on the face of the earth in his day, Moses had to be the one who knew God the best. His experience of God, and his intimacy with God, far surpassed any other in that generation. But God did something so surprising, so astounding, that it caused Moses to pray a very strange prayer, one that you would never have expected to come from him.

WHO IN THE WORLD WAS MOSES?

Moses was brought up in the court of Pharaoh, the king of Egypt. He had been adopted as a baby by Pharaoh's daughter. She had hired Moses' own mother to care for him (Exodus chapters 2–3). Many scholars think that he was likely the next in line for the throne of Egypt, and Egypt, in Moses' day, was the greatest kingdom in the world.

But Moses was an Israelite, not an Egyptian, and the Israelites were all slaves to the Egyptians, and had been in bondage to Egypt for almost four hundred years. His mother had obviously taught him who he was, and Who his God was. This is evident in Scripture:

> By faith Moses, when he became of age, re-
> fused to be called the son of Pharaoh's daugh-
> ter, choosing rather to suffer affliction with the
> people of God than to enjoy the passing plea-
> sures of sin, esteeming the reproach of Christ
> greater riches than the treasures of Egypt; for
> he looked to the reward. (Hebrews 11:24–26)

Don't you think that for a young man to make that kind
of a decision and to make that kind of a sacrifice, he really had
to know and love his God? I have no doubt that Moses really
knew and loved God greatly, for he rejected all that Egypt offered and identified himself as an Israelite, and thus became a
slave–laborer.

But eventually he killed an Egyptian for abusing one of his
Israelite brothers, so he had to flee the country. He ended up
in the Sinai wilderness, tending someone else's flock of sheep
for forty years.

THE BURNING BUSH

At the end of the forty years, as he was tending the sheep in the
desert, he saw a bush burning, but it was not being consumed.
So he went to look at this strange sight, and a voice from heav-
en said, *"Take your sandals off your feet, for the place where you
stand is holy ground"* (Exodus 3:5).

God then told Moses to go back to Egypt to set the people of Israel free from slavery, and to bring them back to the
mountain on which he was then standing (Mount Sinai). And
God also promised to take them to their own "promised land."

Then Moses asked God what His name was. And God answered that it was Yahweh (Jehovah), which is Hebrew, mean-ing "I AM WHO I AM" (Exodus 3:1–14), and is translated in the English Bible as "the LORD" or "GOD" (spelled in all up-percase letters). Thus God revealed Himself to Moses by a spe-cial name that He had never before recorded in His Scriptures (Exodus 6:3).

This was a marvelous encounter with God. Moses actually heard God's voice, stood in God's Presence, was given a special name for God, and received a special commission from God.

LIBERATION!

So Moses went back to Egypt and, by many miracles that God performed through him, he liberated the Israelites from the bondage of slavery. This man really knew God. He was used mightily by God, and God spoke to him regularly and clearly. He knew God's voice. He was very intimate with God. He knew how to talk to God, and how to hear Him. He saw God's power demonstrated in the plagues unleashed upon Egypt that even-tually set his people, Israel, free (Exodus chapters 4–13).

Then God, through Moses, led this ragtag bunch of freed slaves out into the desert, with all their belongings and the riches of Egypt (for they had plundered the Egyptians) piled on their backs, their animals, and their carts. They headed out to the "land flowing with milk and honey," which God had promised them.

God provided a pillar of cloud over them every day (great shade), and a pillar of fire over them every night (great street lighting). God miraculously parted the water of the Red Sea and they walked through it on dry ground. Then God let the water flood back in, destroying Pharaoh's army, which was pursuing them.

They soon ran out of food, so He provided, on six days of every week, a bread–like substance called "manna" for them to eat. They came to a place where the water was bitter, and God miraculously made it fresh. From this time on, wherever they journeyed, God provided a rock from which gushed enough pure water to satisfy all the people and their animals. In this way, God miraculously led them, fed them, watered them, and cared for them (Exodus chapters 14–17).

By following the pillar of cloud, God led them to Mount Sinai, where Moses had seen the burning bush, and they camped at the base of the mountain. God then told Moses that they must obey His voice and keep His covenant. In three days, He would speak to them from the top of the mountain; Moses was to tell them to get ready (Exodus 19:1–15). And the people replied, *"All that the Lord has spoken we will do"* (Exodus 19:8).

THE VOICE THAT CAUSED AN EARTHQUAKE

On the third day, the mountain became enveloped with thick cloud. There was lightning and thunder, and the Lord descended upon it in fire and thick smoke. The whole mountain shook, and from it there came the blast of a trumpet that grew louder and louder (Exodus 19:16–19). Then there came from the mountain, a tremendous, thunderous Voice speaking to them. It was God's audible Voice. Absolutely awesome!

This Voice was so powerful that it caused an earthquake. The ground shook and the people trembled greatly. And even Moses was exceedingly afraid and trembling. Never before had

God spoken so powerfully and clearly. The voice of God came thundering down, giving them the great Ten Commandments:

> I am the LORD your God…
> You shall have no other gods before [besides] Me.
> You shall not make for yourself a carved image—any likeness of anything… you shall not bow down to them nor serve them…
> You shall not take the name of the LORD your God in vain…
> Remember [observe] the Sabbath day, to keep it holy…
> Honor your father and your mother…
> You shall not murder.
> You shall not commit adultery.
> You shall not steal.
> You shall not bear false witness [lie] against your neighbor.
> You shall not covet… (Exodus 20:2–5, 7–8, 12–17)

The people were so terrified and overwhelmed that when God finished speaking, they ran to Moses and said to him, *"You speak with us, and we will hear; but let not God speak with us, lest we die"* (Exodus 20:19).

So Moses went up onto Mount Sinai—into the cloud, the smoke, the fire, the thunder, and the lightning. He was there with God for forty days and forty nights, and he talked "face to face" with God (Exodus 33:11). He couldn't see God, but he heard Him, as if they were talking face to face.

During those forty days, God gave Moses two tablets of stone, and on the tablets, with His own finger, God engraved the same Ten Commandments He had previously spoken to the Israelites in that terrifying, thunderous voice. No one else ever had such an awesome and intimate experience with God as Moses did up there on that mountain (Exodus 32:15–16).

Oops, a Disaster!

Meanwhile, near the end of those forty days, the people began to wonder whether their leader, Moses, had been struck by the lightning on the mountain. So they made a golden calf and began worshiping it, eating and drinking to it, singing and shouting to it, and dancing before it. It was likely a bull–calf, because that had been one of the gods of Egypt. And being a bull–calf, it was likely representative of sexual and fertility rites. This was quite likely a drunken, sexual orgy, and many of the people were involved (Exodus 32:1–14).

Remember that just forty days before, they had heard God's thunderous voice saying, *"I am the LORD your God… You shall have no other gods before [besides] Me. You shall not make for yourself a carved image—any likeness of anything… you shall not bow down to them nor serve them"* (Exodus 20:2–5). But now the Israelites were quickly and blatantly breaking the commandments God had spoken to them so powerfully.

Suddenly, God broke off the conversation with Moses and told him to get down off the mountain because the people were corrupting themselves. So Moses picked up the two tablets of stone and started down the mountain. He got near the camp and saw the people worshiping this idolatrous golden calf and dancing around it, completely unrestrained.

Moses was so disgusted and angry that he threw the stone

tablets to the ground, breaking them. He ran into the camp, and shouted, *"Whoever is on the LORD's side—come to me!"* (Exodus 32:26). He told those who came to get their swords and to kill every man who was involved in this idolatrous worship, this drunken orgy, even if it was their own friend or brother (Exodus 32:19–28).

The party was over. There was a big slaughter; about three thousand people were killed. Those who were left must have begun to realize the terrible thing they had done against God.

SURPRISE, SURPRISE!

But wonder of wonders, the pillar of cloud did not leave. The pillar of fire stayed all night. The manna was there in the morning as usual. The rock was still issuing that beautiful, cool, clear water just like before. God had not left. He was still there. He was still providing and caring for them. This is astonishing! I am amazed at this. Aren't you? Listen to what the Word of God says about it. This is the little-known side of God's astounding nature:

> But You are God,
> Ready to pardon,
> Gracious and merciful,
> Slow to anger,
> Abundant in kindness,
> And did not forsake them.
> Even when they made a molded calf for themselves,
> And said, 'This is your god
> That brought you up out of Egypt,'
> And worked great provocations,

Yet in Your manifold mercies
You did not forsake them in the wilderness.
The pillar of cloud did not depart from them by day,
To lead them on the road;
Nor the pillar of fire by night,
To show them light,
And the way they should go.
You also gave Your good Spirit to instruct them,
And did not withhold Your manna from their mouth,
And gave them water for their thirst.
Forty years You sustained them in the wilderness;
They lacked nothing... (Nehemiah 9:17–21)

AN ASTONISHING REQUEST

It was the next day that Moses prayed his very surprising prayer. He said to God, *"Now therefore, I pray, if I have found grace in Your sight, show me now Your way, that I may know You..."* (Exodus 33:13).

Then Moses asked God for something more astonishing: *"Please, show me Your glory"* (Exodus 33:18).

Moses, what do you mean, asking to know God and see His glory? Why are you asking that? You saw the burning bush that was not consumed. You saw all the miracles, plagues, and judgments unleashed upon Egypt. You saw the pillar of cloud and the pillar of fire. You saw the parting of the Red Sea and the destruction of Pharaoh's army. You saw the manna, and the rock giving water. You saw the terrible sight of Mount Sinai engulfed with thick cloud, smoke, and fire. You saw the whole mountain shake violently. You heard the thunderings, the trumpet blasts, and the terrifying, awesome voice of God. You felt the ground shake. You went up and saw the finger of God engraving the tablets of stone. For forty days you spoke face to face with Him. What more do you want? Haven't you already seen His glory?

This is very surprising. Knowing God so well already, why did he pray, *"God, I want to know You. Please show me Your glory"*?

WHAT KIND OF GOD IS THIS?

Well, after all the idolatry and debauchery, Moses must have been expecting the wrath and judgment of God to fall on them. But instead of wrath, he saw the pillar of cloud and fire still with them, the manna on the ground just as before, and the rock still pouring out fresh water. He must have said to himself, *After what these people have done, God is still here. He hasn't left. He is still providing for us, and still blessing us. What kind of God is this? I didn't know He was like this. I've seen His power. I've seen His miracles. I've seen His judgments. I've heard His voice. But this is a side of God I didn't know existed. Oh God, show me more of who You really are.*

Suppose you had been there. Would you really expect the pillar of cloud to remain? Would you expect that pillar of fire to stay overhead throughout the night? Would you take your basket out the next morning, expecting the manna to be there as before? Would you take your bucket out to the rock, confident that the water would be flowing just like yesterday? I don't think I would have expected God to stay and bless us. Wouldn't we be saying to ourselves, *After the way we have bro-*

ken God's commandments so terribly, surely He will punish us and depart from us. We are surely in trouble now!

For many years, I thought I knew a lot about God. I knew He *"so loved the world that He gave His only begotten Son, that whoever believes in Him should not perish but have everlasting life"* (John 3:16). But I thought of Him as being The Heavenly Policeman or The Great Judge: cold, stern, harsh, hating sin, reluctant to forgive, eager to punish, and hard to please. I didn't know God was so wonderfully merciful, gracious, forgiving, and good. My knowledge of this side of God was terribly lacking and very unbalanced. What about your concept of God? Has it been similar to the view of God I had?

I have found that most non–Christians, as well as many Christians, don't know that God is so wonderfully good. They don't know God is so merciful, so gracious, so patient, so forgiving, so kind, and so compassionate. They, too, would have expected thunderbolts, judgment, and fire coming down on such an idolatrous orgy.

Yes, God did judge the Israelites' sin, but because Moses interceded for them, God was very willing to forgive them, stay with them, and keep on providing for them (Exodus 32:31–33:17). He still loved them.

Do you want to know what God's Heart and nature are truly like? The good news is that *He eagerly wants to show Himself and His goodness to us*—more and more and more. He is much more willing than we are. We just need to ask Him, just like Moses did. That is all that Moses did; he just asked— and God answered.

GOD'S AWESOME GOODNESS

But when Moses asked, *"Please, show me Your glory,"* God instead answered, *"I will make all My goodness pass before you..."* (Exodus 33:18–19).

This difference in wording is extremely important. God is not being careless with His words here. He never is. God is telling us that *His greatest glory is His goodness.* It's not His power, although His power is awesome. His goodness is more amazing, more wonderful, more astounding, more precious, and more enthralling than even His great power. There is nothing more glorious than the absolute, unchanging goodness and true love of God.

The word "good" means high and true moral character, benevolent, beneficial, advantageous, favorable, profitable, best welfare (in the widest sense), kind, merciful, gracious, compassionate, gentle, perfect, and excellent.

God is telling us that His goodness is His glory. Do you get the picture? This is our first glimpse into the Heart of God. He is incredibly, absolutely, eternally good, because He is love.

> The LORD is good to all, and His tender mercies are over all His works. (Psalm 145:9)

> Oh, give thanks to the LORD, for He is good! For His mercy endures forever. (Psalm 106:1)

> For You, LORD, are good, and ready [eager] to forgive, and abundant in mercy to all those who call upon You. (Psalm 86:5)

Oh, how great is Your goodness, which You have laid up for those who fear [revere] You, which You have prepared for those who trust in You. (Psalm 31:19)

Oh, taste and see that the LORD is good; blessed is the man [person] who trusts in Him! (Psalm 34:8)

Would you like to know more of the glorious goodness and astounding love of God? I don't mean just an intellectual head-knowledge, but an actual ever-growing heart-experience and life-changing reality of His great goodness and amazing true love. More than anything else in the world, I personally yearn for a greater, growing experience of Him and His immeasurable love.

LABELS ARE IMPORTANT—BUT THEY ARE ONLY LABELS

Then, strangely, God said to Moses that He would *"proclaim the name of the LORD"* (Exodus 33:19). Why would God say that? He had already proclaimed His name, "Yahweh" (the LORD), at the burning bush.

Here is the reason. At the burning bush, God gave Moses one of His names—like a label on a bottle. But now, because Moses has asked to really know Him, God is going to reveal what is inside the bottle, not just what's on the label. God is going to proclaim His real Heart and His true, loving inner nature—Who He truly is.

Let me illustrate what I mean. When you need to take

an aspirin, do you go to the aspirin bottle and peel off the label, wad it up, and swallow it? No? Why not? It says "Aspirin," doesn't it? Yes, it says "Aspirin," but the label is only a description of what is really inside the bottle. It's the *real* thing inside that you want. Now, a label must be a true and accurate description of what is inside, but just taking the label alone can't help you. You need to receive (experience) the real thing inside.

So whenever God reveals any of His names, He is actually revealing who He is, and what He is really like inside. But the name itself is only just a label. When Scripture mentions "the name of the LORD," it is actually speaking of the nature and character of God, the very essence of His Being. Don't be fascinated with just His names (the labels), but receive the real God that the label describes.

I want to know God more and more, because the more I get to know Him and experience His goodness and love, the more I am filled with awe and amazement at how wonderful He is. And it makes me want to know Him even better.

You can experience Him, too. He desires that for you, and for all of us. In fact, He is more willing to reveal Himself to you than you are to know and experience Him. You may have heard that "God is love," but have you received His amazing love deep inside your heart?

LET'S ASK HIM:

> God, I want to really know You. If others can know You, why can't I? Please reveal Yourself to me. Show me what You are like inside—Your very loving Heart.
>
> Take away my fears. Open my heart to Yours. Let the entrance of Your Word enlighten my understanding. Take away all the wrong concepts I have of You.
>
> Give me the true, full picture of who You are, and what You really are, deep within Your Heart.
>
> I ask this in the power of Jesus' name.

CHAPTER TWO

GOD'S AWESOME ANSWER: HIS GREAT GOODNESS

God Reveals His Amazing Inner Heart to Us

GOD OPENS WIDE HIS HEART

Remember when Moses said, *"Please, show me Your glory,"* God instead answered, *"I will make all My goodness pass before you."* This means that God's greatest glory is His wonderful Heart of goodness and true love.

This is how God revealed His goodness to Moses. God told Moses to come up on the mountain again, and He said:

> I will make all My goodness pass before you,
> and I will proclaim the name [the nature and
> character] of the LORD before you... You can-
> not see My face; for no man shall see Me, and
> live... So it shall be, while My glory passes by,
> that I will put you in the cleft of the rock, and
> will cover you with My hand while I pass by.
> Then I will take away My hand, and you shall
> see My back; but My face shall not be seen. (Ex-
> odus 33:19–20, 22–23)

When Moses got up there, God put him in the cleft of the rock, covered over the cave with His hand, and *"the LORD*

descended in the cloud and stood with him [Moses] there, and
proclaimed the name [the nature and character] of the Lord"
(Exodus 34:5).

This is the first time recorded in Scripture that God opened up His Heart and revealed to the human race His nature, character, disposition, and temperament. Notice that this is God Himself telling us what He is, deep inside Himself—what the very essence of His Being really is. This is not man telling us what God is like. *This is God telling man what God is like.* This is the most direct and explicit revelation about His inner nature that God had ever revealed in Scripture up to that time.

All through the book of Genesis and the book of Exodus up to this point, God had only revealed Himself as the Creator, the Almighty One, the Self–Existent One, the Eternal One, the Supreme One, the Sovereign Ruler, the Judge of All the Earth, the God of Heaven and Earth, the God Who Sees, the God Who Provides, and the Lord (Yahweh).

Not until Exodus 22:27 does God give us the first glimpse into His inner Heart, when He says, *"I am gracious [full of grace]."* But here in Exodus 34:5–7, God opens up and conveys to us His nature, character, and disposition—His real Heart, the very center of His Being—*all His goodness.*

Now let's take a look at what God revealed to Moses up there on the mountain.

The Glory of God: All of His Great Goodness

And the Lord passed before him [Moses] and proclaimed, "The Lord, the Lord God, merci-

ful [full of mercy] and gracious [full of grace], longsuffering [full of patience], and abounding in goodness and truth, keeping mercy for thousands, forgiving iniquity and transgression and sin, by no means clearing the guilty..."
(Exodus 34:6–7)

God said, audibly, "The LORD [Yahweh], the LORD [Yahweh] God." (Yahweh is a Hebrew word meaning "I AM WHO I AM.") God is saying, "I'm showing you Who I AM: My Glory—all My goodness—My real Heart." He is saying:

I AM God.
 I AM full of mercy.
  I AM full of grace.
   I AM full of patience.
    I AM overflowing with goodness.
     I AM overflowing with truth.
      I AM faithful to keep My covenant of mercy.
       I AM eager to forgive every kind of sin.
        I AM also full of justice.

The great Ten Commandments that God had spoken previously (Exodus 20:1–17) reveal God's main standards for human behavior. But they do not give us much insight into God's wonderful love and goodness—His Heart. When God spoke those Ten Commandments, Moses and the people were very afraid and trembled.

But when God spoke these eight great traits of Who He really is, deep inside His Heart, God's glory came upon Moses, whose face was still shining like the sun forty days later when he came down from the mountain to the people (Exodus 34:29–35). What a great difference there is between these two proclamations and the responses they produce. God's law produces fear, but God's grace produces glory. The revelation of God's inner Heart is much more glorious than the revelation of God's external commandments—the law.

These eight great foundational truths that God proclaims about Himself are simple but very profound. A child can begin to understand them, and yet learned men cannot plumb the full depths of their scope and meaning. The goodness and love of God far surpass human knowledge and comprehension. Yet they are available for us to receive, increasingly experience, and enjoy as we grow spiritually:

> [that you] may be able to comprehend with all the saints [believers] what is the width and length and depth and height—to know the love of Christ [God's love through Him] which passes knowledge; that you may be filled with all the fullness of God. (Ephesians 3:18–19)

It was because Moses asked, "I want to know You," that we are now able to see the *true* Heart—the nature, the character, and the temperament of God—as never before. This was a new side, a new revelation, a new insight into the Heart of the great, eternal, sovereign, almighty Creator of heaven and earth. And this was freely given just because Moses asked. He didn't have to work for it, earn it, figure it out, merit it, or deserve it in any way. God eagerly revealed Himself by His great loving grace to Moses—for us all.

A Closer Look at God's Great Goodness

Let's go back and take a closer look at those eight marvelous truths that God declared about Himself (Exodus 34:6–7).
(We will look at them in much more detail in Chapters 9 and
10.) Remember that He called these wonderful truths "all My
goodness," and He called His goodness "His glory."

God Is Full of Mercy

Note that God is full of mercy—not partially full, but totally
full. Every part of His Being is full of mercy. It permeates every
part of Him. What is mercy? Very simply, "mercy" means *not*
getting the judgment and punishment that we rightly deserve.
The Hebrew word here also means full of pity, love, tenderness,
compassion, sympathy, affection, care, and sensitivity. This is
what our great Creator truly is, in His innermost Being. I am
extremely glad that He is like this. What if He were unmerciful
and wanted to give us the punishment we really deserve? If He
were, we all would have been "ash in a flash" a long time ago.
Many people don't know that He is so good, so loving, and so
merciful. They think He is hard, harsh, and waiting to punish
them.

God Is Full of Grace

Here again, note that God is totally full of grace—every part
of Him. "Grace" means getting the favor, goodness, and
blessing that we do *not* deserve. Mercy and grace are like
twin sisters—two sides of the same coin. He is kind and generous, and always beneficent. He gives far more goodness

than we deserve. God is so wonderful! Yes, He is much more than wonderful. He is utterly astounding! Most people I have met don't know that He genuinely wants to abundantly bless them and do them great good—even when they don't deserve it.

God Is Longsuffering

"Longsuffering" simply means that God is patient, slow to anger. He is not quick–tempered, irritable, or cranky. He is not easily provoked. He does not lose His temper. He bears with us for a long, long time before He takes corrective action. If He wasn't longsuffering, we surely would have been "ash in a flash" long ago. For many years, I thought He was just the opposite of patient. I didn't know this side of God. Now I know differently. I am so thankful He is so incredibly patient. I hope you also are beginning to realize this, too.

God Overflows with Goodness

This goes beyond mercy and grace. God pours out abundantly to us that which is beneficial, profitable, advantageous, favorable, wholesome, and excellent. He is benevolent, kind, and perfectly righteous. His goodness is greater than we can ever imagine. I greatly rejoice in this. I love Him for all that He is in the very center of His Heart.

God Overflows with Truth

God is *totally* true, authentic, genuine, and right. He cannot lie. He cannot deceive. He is so full of truth that He pours out abundantly to us every bit of truth we need. He is the God who speaks, who communicates, who reveals Himself, and who leads us into all truth. We can absolutely trust Him, everything that He says, and all that He has written in His Word, because He is true. How wonderful!

God Faithfully Keeps His Promises

God faithfully keeps His covenants and His promises. He cannot break them. He cannot fail to do what He has spoken or what He has written. He is *absolutely* faithful. This concept is emphasized in Deuteronomy 7:9: *"...the LORD your God, He is God, the faithful God who keeps covenant and mercy for a thousand generations with those who love Him and keep His commandments."* This is extremely good news for us all.

God Forgives Iniquity, Transgression, and Sin

"To forgive" means to lift off all guilt or blame, to pardon, to withdraw the charges, to cease to demand the penalty. God uses three different Hebrew words here: *avon* (iniquity), *pesha* (transgression), and *chattaah* (sin). "Iniquity" means perversity, deviation from what is right. "Transgression" means rebellion, breaking the bounds, trespassing. "Sin" means to miss the mark, to break the law, to offend. These three words cover the whole range of our human sin, failure, and wrongdoing.

God is eager and willing to forgive it all, because He sent His Son, Jesus, to completely pay the penalty for all our sin on His cross. This is God's true nature, His disposition, and His Heart. This is the very center and essence of His Being. He cannot be anything else. He offers full forgiveness to everyone for everything that they have ever done wrong, if they will wholeheartedly turn back to Him, ask, and receive. This is the greatest of all good news for imperfect, sinning people like us. I am extremely glad and deeply grateful to God for His wonderful, complete, free forgiveness. I hope you are, too.

God Is Full of Justice

Then, after pronouncing all of the above, God said that He will *"by no means [clear/justify] the guilty"* (Exodus 34:7). Hey! Wait a minute! God just finished saying that He would forgive all sin. Is God contradicting Himself? No, He cannot! Then what does He mean?

Think this through with me. If God offers forgiveness to every person, for every sin, then who is left guilty? The answer has to be those who refuse to accept God's offer and provision of forgiveness. What else could it mean? For, you see, forgiveness is neither automatic nor forced. If we refuse His forgiveness, God cannot clear our guilt. He will not force His forgiveness on anyone. God's forgiveness must be willingly and deliberately received by faith. If we reject, or just neglect, to receive His forgiveness on His terms, we will remain guilty, and He cannot clear us of our guilt. It will certainly be *our* choice—not His.

God very much wants to forgive us. That is His genuine nature and His Heart's earnest desire. In His mercy, grace, and love, God has provided a way by which we all can be forgiven and saved from the guilt and punishment of all our sin. But if we reject, or even just neglect, God's mercy, grace, longsuffering, goodness, truth, and forgiveness, we remain guilty by our own choice. This will *not* be God's will; it will be our own proud, stubborn, and foolish rebellion. God will not force His forgiveness upon us. That would violate the free will that He lovingly created within us.

THE GREAT BALANCING ACT

Yes, God is full of mercy, grace, goodness, and forgiveness, but He is also full of absolute truth, justice, and righteousness. There is justice in the universe. God created it that way. The Scriptures teach that wrong must be righted. Injustice must be recompensed. Evil must be punished. The whole physical realm is based on exact and precise laws of nature. So, also, is the whole spiritual realm. Those who say, "There is no absolute truth, no final authority. Everything is relative. It's just what you think, or want to think," are wrong—dead wrong. There is no basis for them to say that. It is just wishful thinking— deadly wishful thinking.

What kind of a God would He be if He let all the horrible atrocities, the heinous violations of justice, and the cruel abuses and vile perversions go completely unrequited? We would consider any judge in our earthly courts to be contemptible if he did nothing about that which is terribly wrong and unjust. God is in perfect balance: He is absolutely just but He is *also* absolutely good, and completely loving and merciful.

From these eight wonderful proclamations of God's great goodness, we gain the insight that there are two sides to God's true character and nature. On one side, there is love (mercy, grace, patience, goodness, and forgiveness), and on the other side, there is justice (truth, faithfulness, and righteousness). At first glance, these two sides may look like they are contrary to each other. But they are not. They are marvelously and inextricably harmonized together. Later, in Chapters 7 and 13, we will see how wonderfully and beautifully these two aspects (sides) of God's nature are perfectly blended together.

HUNGRY AND THIRSTY FOR MORE OF GOD?

No matter whether you are a believer in God or not, no matter whether you know the Bible or you don't, no matter how much you think you know about God right now, there is so much more of Him yet to know. He is far beyond, and far better than, what you and I can ever imagine—immeasurably so!

I have come to believe, from what I've found out about God so far, that even as we spend eternity with Him, we'll never come to the end of knowing more and more about Him and being astounded and delighted and amazed by Him. I believe that God is infinite. Do you know what "infinite" means? It means that there is no end, no limits, no boundaries. No matter how well you and I know God now, there's much more to discover of His wonderful Heart—right here and now on earth.

PRESSING ON—REACHING FORWARD

Here is another example, this time from the New Testament, of a man who knew God very, very well and yet yearned to know Him much, much more. Look at Paul the apostle. He knew the Scriptures of God very well, but he met Christ in a blinding light and heard His voice on the road to Damascus, and he was radically transformed (Acts 9:1–20). Shortly after that, for three years in the deserts of Arabia, God revealed to him the gospel (good news) of God's grace and Christ's salvation. He became a teacher, a prophet, and an apostle (one sent on a special mission). He went on several extensive missionary journeys, leading thousands to faith in Jesus and establishing thriving churches in many countries. God, through him, wrote much of the New Testament Scriptures. He knew God and was greatly used by God, likely more than any other man of his day.

Yet, near the end of his life, Paul wrote:

> Yet indeed I also count all things loss for the excellence of the knowledge [experience] of Christ Jesus my Lord... and count them as rubbish, that I may gain Christ... that I may know [experience] Him and the power of His resurrection... I press toward the goal for the prize of the upward call of God in Christ Jesus. (Philippians 3:8–10, 14)

This is Paul's way of saying, "More than anything else in all the world, I want to actually experience the highest possible degree of closeness, intimacy, oneness, and union with Jesus, so that I may actually possess and experience much more of Him and the power of His resurrection working through me. I don't know all of Him yet. I haven't quit hungering and thirsting, so I'm reaching out for more and more of Jesus."

Paul knew that Jesus and God the Father are far more wonderful and way beyond everything that he had yet found out about Them. I, too, want to know much more about God and about Jesus. Do you?

Let's Ask Him:

God, please open the eyes of my heart to see how good You really are, and to believe how good You are.

Expand and deepen my understanding of Your mercy, Your grace, Your patience, Your goodness, Your truth, Your faithfulness, Your forgiveness, and Your justice.

Help me not to reject anything that is genuinely You.

Help me to keep Your love and Your justice in proper balance.

God, please give me a healthy hunger and thirst for You, deep within my heart.

I'm not worthy. I don't deserve You. But in Your great mercy and grace, come to me anyway. Show Yourself to me in a way that I can recognize that it is You.

I ask all this in the power of Jesus' name.

CHAPTER THREE

DON'T SWEAT IT—JUST ASK HIM

The Greatest Revealer of God's Heart

WE CAN'T DO IT OURSELVES

Now, I've got to tell you this very important fact before we go any further. Jesus said, *"Nor does anyone know the Father except the Son, and the one to whom the Son wills to reveal Him"* (Matthew 11:27).

This means that we cannot really know, understand, and experience God the Father just by reading, studying, and using our natural minds, our human intellects, and our logic. We cannot know God by our own human ability and effort. If we could figure out God on our own, then the most intelligent and logical persons, the ones with the most education and ability, would have the advantage. That would exclude the rest of us. But God, in His great love for everyone and in His great wisdom, has made Himself available (knowable) to everyone—even to the little children, the disadvantaged, and the simple-minded—all on the same basis: all we have to do is ask Jesus to reveal God to us. How loving and wise God is in this! He totally loves every person equally—every man and woman, every boy and girl, of every nation, tribe, and tongue on earth, rich or poor, learned or unlearned. He passionately loves us all.

HE WILL DO IT FOR US

Getting to know the Father is a supernatural, spiritual process in the hands of Jesus Himself. Jesus is the One, and the *only* One, who can reveal the Father to us, by His Spirit and by His Word, the Bible. He can open the eyes of our understanding—deep within our spirits—deeper than our minds and our natural intellects. We must ask Him, learn from Him, and trust Him to progressively open our hearts and, deep inside, show us God the Father and His great goodness. He is most eager and willing to do this for us.

In John 14:6-7, Jesus said, *"I am the way [to the Father], the truth [about the Father], and the life [of the Father]. No one comes to the Father except through Me. If you had known Me, you would have known My Father also..."* The context of these two verses is the Father and the way to the Father. Jesus is the way!

In Ephesians 1:17-18, Paul prays for believers *"that the God of our Lord Jesus Christ, the Father of glory, may give to you the spirit of wisdom and revelation in the knowledge of Him, the eyes of your understanding being enlightened..."* Paul could not give that to them by himself. He had to ask God to reveal Himself to them. And that is my prayer for you as you read this book.

HE IS THE GOD WHO SPEAKS—SO LET'S LISTEN

One of the main ways God has revealed Himself to the human race is by giving to us the Scriptures, the Word of God. Today, we call it the Bible. He has preserved His Word for thousands of years—right up to this present time. So read the Word of

God and study the Scriptures, asking Jesus to open the eyes of your heart more and more, to see what God is actually like.

God also speaks to our minds. But if we read the Bible, or this book, with just our natural mind and intellect, we will get it wrong and our understanding will be very incomplete and superficial. Yes, use your mind while you read. Think things through. But do more than that. *Listen* also to God's Spirit. His Spirit will open up God's written Word and put His thoughts into your mind. *Open up* deep inside, not to another person, but to the Lord. *Ask* Jesus to reveal the Father to you, in His own way, in His own time, and as progressively as you can handle it. *Trust* Him to do this for you. He has promised. He has sent His Son Jesus, His Spirit, and His Word to do this— for us all.

Hunting with Your Heart

God has written in His Word, "*call upon Me and go and pray to Me, and I will listen to you. And you will seek Me and find Me, when you search for Me with all your heart*" (Jeremiah 29:12–13). God looks for wholeheartedness and sincerity. He will not respond to our half-hearted efforts. Anyone who nonchalantly decides to give God a wee bit of a try, to see if He is what they want Him to be (a consumer attitude), will likely not find Him responsive. But if a person earnestly wants God, and is willing to persistently seek Him and accept Him as Who He really is—and what He is truly like—God has promised that such a person will find Him. In fact, God is eagerly seeking for people who seek Him in this way, and will gladly reveal Himself to them.

The God Who Wants to Be Found

Jesus promised,

> Ask and keep on asking and it shall be given
> you; seek and keep on seeking and you shall
> find; knock and keep on knocking and the
> door shall be opened to you. For everyone who
> asks and keeps on asking receives; and he who
> seeks and keeps on seeking finds; and to him
> who knocks and keeps on knocking the door
> shall be opened. (Luke 11:9–10, AMP)

You see, God is not trying to hide from us or avoid us. He is intensely yearning for us to personally know and experience Him in a very loving and intimate relationship. He wants us far more than we could ever want Him. But He will not sell Himself cheaply. He will be glad to stoop down to us and meet us when we sincerely seek Him with all our heart, and persevere, but He will not devalue or degrade Himself for those who don't really mean business.

It is like a very loving father playing Hide and Seek with his little child. The whole point of the game is the thrill and delight of finding each other. If the child is having difficulty finding him, then Daddy reveals himself in some way or another, and they rush together and embrace. But God is not playing some trivial game. He is very, very serious about this. He knows that it is a matter of life and death for us—eternal life or eternal death—that we find Him and receive Him.

Actual Intimacy with God

The word "know" as used in Scripture has a much deeper meaning than the way we commonly use it today. The first time it is used in Scripture, referring to a personal relationship, is in Genesis 4:1—*"Adam knew Eve his wife, and she conceived and bore Cain."* Obviously, this was not just an abstract realization of some facts about Eve. This was actually experiencing closeness, intimacy, oneness, and union. This is what "know" means most of the time throughout all of Scripture: actual experience, personal relationship. This is what Moses meant when he prayed, *"that I might know You [God]."* This is also what Paul meant when he said, *"that I may know Him [Jesus] and the power of His resurrection…"*—not intellectual theology (head knowledge), but actually experiencing God, and closeness and intimacy with Him.

Let's Ask Him:

> Jesus, I ask that You will make Your Word living and powerful to me, and cause the entrance of Your Word to enlighten my understanding of You.

> Jesus, show me the Father. Send me Your Spirit to reveal the true knowledge of Him.

> Jesus, give me a deeper, fuller, and more accurate concept of who God the Father is, and what He is like.

I don't want just a lot of "head facts." I want to experience God and closeness with Him.

I ask this in all the power and victory of Your name.

CHAPTER FOUR

THE WORLD'S WORST SLANDER

God's Enemy—Hard at Work on All of Us

God is altogether wonderful, infinitely loving, and inconceivably good. But that is not the picture many people all over the world have of Him. They have the very opposite concept of Him being harsh, angry, judgmental, and hard to please. Why is this? What has gone wrong? How did the picture get so twisted?

The answer is that God has been slandered. It is the world's worst slander. God's beautiful, loving character has been maliciously assassinated, viciously twisted, horribly smeared, terribly distorted, and hatefully lied against.

You see, God has an enemy. This enemy is in opposition, in every way, to God and to everything God loves. God calls him *"that serpent of old, called the Devil and Satan, who deceives the whole world"* (Revelation 12:9). God has given this enemy two main names: "satan," which means enemy or opponent; and "devil," which means accuser or slanderer. The devil is the world's most vicious slanderer, a false accuser, and one who maliciously lies about God, about us, and about others—but especially about God.

THE FATHER OF ALL LIES

Jesus said of the devil, *"He was a murderer from the beginning, and does not stand in the truth, because there is no truth in him. When he speaks a lie, he speaks from his own resources, for he is a liar and the father of it"* (John 8:44). This murderer has, for thousands of years, done all he can to assassinate the reputation of the real character and true, loving nature of God, to smear Him and slander Him in every possible way. Whether we are a Christian or not, he has tried to give us a twisted, false, malicious concept of who God is and what He is like.

THE ACCUSER—THE SLANDERER—
THE CHARACTER ASSASSIN

Satan is the accuser of believers, who accuses them before God *"day and night"* (Revelation 12:10). And he also accuses us to one another, causing strife, divisions, and broken relationships.

The devil also accuses God to us. He says things like, "Oh, God is not totally just and righteous. God won't keep all His promises. God doesn't have all power. He can't do what you need. God doesn't really love you. He is just using you for His own selfish purposes."

Here's another slander: "God is just a great big egomaniac up there saying, 'Okay, everybody, submit. Bow down. Worship Me. Praise Me. Tell Me how good I am.'" But this is a huge lie. I've discovered how to answer this. I'll tell you about it when we discuss "The Humility of God" in Chapter 9.

THE DECEIVER—THE TWISTER

The Devil Will Try to Misinterpret the Circumstances of Life to Us

Sometimes we go through hard times, and bad things happen. Then the devil may come along and say something like, "See! God isn't good after all. He's mean. Because you did something sinful, He now hates you. And He is enjoying the chance to punish you. He lied to you. He promised all that blessing and now all you get is trouble. His promises aren't true."

When things are going well for everyone else except you, the devil, very subtly, may whisper these thoughts into your mind, "God doesn't really love you. He's playing favorites. God is not fair. He promised you good, and now look at all the bad stuff you're going through, and everyone else is being blessed. Maybe His promises are true for others, but not for you. God loves other people more than He loves you."

All of those thoughts, those little whispers, those insinuations, are absolutely contrary to the plain statements of the Word of God. They are seductive delusions. They're vicious slanders. They're false accusations. They're cruel deceptions. They're horrible lies. The liar is trying to deceive you. He wants everybody to grow up with some kind of distortion or twist in their concept of what God's nature really is. But Jesus came to show us the truth—the truth about God, the true Loving Father.

The Devil Will Also Try to Twist Scripture

Satan will distort the truth. He knows the Bible well, but Jesus said there is no truth in him. So whenever he quotes Scripture, it is always to pervert it by misinterpreting it, misquoting it, or only partially quoting it. He did that to Jesus in the temptation in the wilderness. But Jesus answered him every time with correct quotations from God's Word, and thus defeated him (Matthew 4:1–11). If satan tries that on you, look up the Scripture and read it and its context. Pray and ask God to show you the truth.

For years, as I read through the Word of God, the devil would underline and highlight in my mind, all of God's wrath and His judgments. At the same time, he seemed to make me blind to God's love and goodness. Then, when God began in that movie theater (did you read the Introduction?) to open my eyes to His grace, His goodness, and His great true love, I started to see that in every instance where there was judgment there also was, previous to that judgment, very much grace, patience, mercy, and many chances for repentance and forgiveness.

The devil will give only partial Scripture, and use it out of context. A half–truth is much more dangerous than a total lie, because there is enough truth in it to sound good and deceive you. Remember that the other half of a half–truth is a lie. If it is only a partial picture, it is a distortion and a twist, lacking the complete balance of truth.

For example, when satan tempted Eve, he began by only partially quoting God's words. Then he questioned what God had said. Then He contradicted what God had said. And then he insinuated that God was not being totally good, and that God was mean and was withholding something good from them. Finally he offered to be "more good" to them than God (Genesis 3:1–5).

The Devil Will Also Try to Distort and Pervert God–Given Role Models

God has established role models to represent Him on earth, and to demonstrate what He is truly like. The main role model is in the family unit. God says that He is our Heavenly Father and we are His children.

This is very important. When God created us, He said to Himself, *"Let Us make man [humans] in Our image, according to Our likeness"* (Genesis 1:26). This is a perfect description of "children." God is the Father, the pattern for fatherhood. So earthly fathers are to be in His image and His likeness, and are to portray His true Heart and nature to their children. Our earthly fathers were meant to demonstrate and model what our Heavenly Father is truly like.

Therefore, the devil works overtime to corrupt fathers and mothers, to twist them, to bend them out of shape, to pervert them, to make them exactly the opposite to what God is really like, so that there will be whole generations that grow up thinking, "If that's God, who wants Him? If that's what God is like, no thanks!"

To the degree that our earthly fathers and mothers portrayed a distorted role model to us, we will likely have a distorted concept of, a wrong fear of, and an aversion to God, our Heavenly Father. To the degree that our concept of God, our

Heavenly Father, is incomplete, distorted, or perverted, our concept and model of what we as earthly fathers and mothers should be, will be incomplete, distorted, or perverted.

To varying degrees, the devil has done that to our dads and moms, and is trying to do that to those of us who are now parents. He's worked very hard to make fathers unloving, uncaring, unaffectionate, cold, harsh, demanding, mean, stingy, selfish, and even abusive, so that people will grow up thinking of that ugliness whenever they hear the word "Father" as referring to God. Because of this, people will turn away from God. This is satan's goal: to turn people away from God, and into an eternity without God—dying guilty, unforgiven, condemned, and lost.

So How Can We Know the Truth?

Even though the devil has done all that twisting and distorting, the grace of God has a remedy for it. God *can* straighten out the bent, twisted, perverted concepts we have of "father." The Word of God *can* pierce the darkness, turn on the light, and expose the lies, deceptions, and slanders. And then you *can* begin to see what the real Heavenly Father is like, not the way you were brought up to think of "father." God's Spirit *can* do this. Jesus *can* heal, not only our bodies but more importantly our minds, our spirits, our souls, our emotions, our wounds, and our hurts. He *can* heal our memories and our past. This is not too hard for Him. Jesus very much wants to show the real Father to us. He wants to bring us to the Father. He says to us today, "Come, I want to introduce you to My great loving Heavenly Father. I came to demonstrate Him to you, to teach you about Him and reveal Him to you, deep inside your spirit, and reconcile you to Him."

WE STAND AT THE CROSSROADS

We are faced with a choice. Believing is a matter of choice. We choose what we believe. So who are you going to believe? Are you going to believe what God says about Himself in His Word, and through Jesus? Or are you going to believe the slanders, the lies, the malicious insinuations, and the character assassinations that the devil tries to feed you?

Do you want to say to Jesus, "Lord, show me the Father"? He will be *delighted* to do so.

Or do you want to say, "No thanks! I'd rather stay away from Him. I'm afraid of Him"? Saying that will break God's Heart, and also the Heart of Jesus. Decide in your heart to say, "Lord Jesus, please show me the Father—the real Father" (see John 14:6–9).

I have found that God is absolutely as good as He says He is and that every one of those slanders that satan has whispered to me about God are absolutely wrong. They are all lies. I love God more now than I have ever loved Him before, because I keep seeing more of how wonderful and loving He really is. And I want this to happen to you, too.

LET'S ASK HIM:

> Lord Jesus, open the eyes of my understanding that I may be able to see the real truth about the Father.

Please erase every wrong concept, every distortion, and every lie about Him. Take away every fear.

Heal my soul, my emotions, my hurts, and my past.

Help me to believe Your Word instead of believing the devil's lies. Show me God's goodness and true love.

Please answer me out of Your great love, in the power of Your name, Jesus.

CHAPTER FIVE

Is God Really Flawless? Or Is He Faulty?

Can We Always Trust Him?

Is God Full of Wholeness— or Full of Holes?

This is a very, very important question. The answer determines whether or not we can put our complete, unwavering trust in God. Our faith hinges on this. It will affect our entire life. It will leave us fearful and shaky—or confident and secure.

God is either holy or holey, a God we can totally trust or a God we cannot always truly depend on. We must find out which is true. Our faith in a holy God can be a solid anchor for our lives—without it, we will be tossed back and forth on the fickle waves of fortune.

Don't Be Afraid of the Word "Holy"

Here is a word the Bible uses frequently. What is the true meaning of this word, "holy"? It has been corrupted and diminished greatly in the English language. Most of the time when people use the word "holy," they mean super-good or even sinless, super-pious, very religious, and keeping a lot of very strict rules. That is a misunderstanding of the complete meaning of the word. In English, the word "holy" comes from the word "whole," meaning total, entire, complete, intact, undiminished, undivided; having all the essential parts, making a perfect unity.

Also, in Greek (in the New Testament) and in Hebrew (in the Old Testament), the root of "holy" means whole, complete, entire, totality, nothing lacking, nothing missing, absolutely pure, absolutely perfect in every way. That is the very basic root meaning of the word "holy." Rather than the negative connotation that many people ascribe to it, "holy" is a very positive, comprehensive, and beautiful word.

GOD IS TOTAL PERFECTION
AND PERFECT TOTALITY

The prophet Isaiah saw a vision of God seated on His throne in Heaven. And around the throne were special angels shouting:

> Holy, holy, holy is the LORD of hosts; the whole
> earth is full of His glory! (Isaiah 6:3)

In the book of Revelation, we again see the throne of God with the highest angels around it, shouting continually:

> Holy, holy, holy, Lord God Almighty, Who was
> and is and is to come! (Revelation 4:8)

In other words, they are continually saying, "God, the Almighty Creator, is whole, entire, complete, pure, undefiled, undiminished, undiluted, absolute perfection."

The Scriptures say again and again that God is Holy—absolutely, infinitely, completely perfect. God is one complete harmonious whole—perfectly integrated, perfectly balanced, perfectly complete—all the time, forever. This is eternal truth. It is God's Word.

> Who is like You, O LORD, among the gods? Who is like You, glorious in holiness... (Exodus 15:11)

> ...God is light [truth and righteousness] and in Him is no darkness at all. (1 John 1:5)

> No one is holy like the LORD... (1 Samuel 2:2)

> Who shall not fear [revere] You, O Lord, and glorify Your name? For You alone are holy. (Revelation 15:4)

God, and only God, is absolutely perfect. He is infinitely perfect. He is eternally perfect. He is the perfect totality and the total perfection. To put it in plain language, God is *everything* that God can be, could ever be, or should ever be. There is *nothing* about Him that is lacking, nothing missing, nothing diluted, nothing polluted, nothing wrong.

He couldn't be anything more than what He already is, because He is the absolute, infinite, eternal, fullness of totality and perfection. He has always been that, and He always will be. He cannot be anything less. This is the full meaning of "Holy is the Lord."

The holiness of God embraces His entire Being—everything He is: every aspect of all His attributes, strengths, abilities, character traits, thoughts, actions, and emotions.

Now, don't be afraid. When the Bible applies the word

"holy" to humans, places, or objects, it does not mean we have to be absolutely perfect like God. It means we are to be wholly dedicated, totally consecrated, and entirely set apart for God and for Him alone—wholeheartedly and completely given to Him and to His purposes alone (even in our imperfections).

ALL–OUT WAR ON OUR FAITH IN GOD

All this may be easy for us to say and believe when things are going nicely and smoothly, but we live in a dirty, cruel, hard, twisted, crooked world. And when things get tough and life serves us a hard blow, satan will start hammering us with some of his lies: "God is failing you. He's not being loving. He's not being fair. He's not being kind and compassionate. He's not being righteous and just. He's not being patient. He's not being good to you. He is not perfect."

The slanderer, both God's enemy and ours, will attack our belief and confidence in God's completeness and perfection. He will do everything in his power to undermine that, to make us doubt it, to shake our faith in God, and to make us become angry at God, because God is not doing things *our* way or according to *our* time schedule, or not giving us exactly what *we* want or precisely what *we* like.

But in God there is not a flaw, not an error, not a failure—nothing missing, nothing lacking. Believe what God says about Himself in His Word. Don't believe the circumstances of life that seem to say the opposite. Don't believe the dirty tricks that satan pulls on you. Don't believe his lies, his insinuations, his dirty slanders. Don't believe his efforts to undermine your faith in the totally holy and loving God. Satan is trying to take

God away from you—the real God, the perfect God, the loving God. Don't let satan steal your faith and confidence in the
infinitely holy and loving God.

VICTORY IS NOT LETTING GO OF GOD

God allowed satan to test a man named Job almost to the point
of death by taking away his wealth, his family, and his health.
But in the midst of it all, Job said, *"Though He [God] slay me,
yet will I trust Him"* (Job 13:15). Job kept on believing in God.
So, in the end, satan was completely defeated, because Job
never rejected or cursed God, even though he came close to it.
He kept on trusting. Soon after this, God restored Job's health
and family, and gave him twice as many possessions as he had
before (Job 42:10–13).

It's not easy to keep trusting God in the midst of difficulties, but once you get to that decision, once you make that
your determination, it does something inside of you. It says
to satan, "It doesn't matter what you do to me, or what you
try. Whatever happens, I've got God, and I'm not letting go of
Him. I'm still going to trust Him and love Him. Satan, you will
lose this battle, and God and I will win!"

This kind of faith is a gift from God. Only God's Spirit can
empower us to make that decision and to stick to it, but God's
Spirit will not make our decision for us. We have to decide of our
own free will. Then He will enable us and empower us to keep
on trusting God when things get difficult. Why not make that
decision in your heart right now? Ask God to help you to believe, and to give you this faith. Say something like this to God:

God, this is what I really want. I want that kind of faith. I want that kind of belief and the confidence that You are absolutely holy and faithful and cannot do anything wrong. I want a determination to live steadfastly trusting You, even in the midst of difficulties. Please give me this kind of faith and develop it within me, more and more, by Your Spirit.

Defeat Is Turning Away From God

The alternative to this victory of faith is to say, "If God doesn't treat me the way *I* think He ought to, if God doesn't do what *I* want, if God allows me to suffer and makes me go through some tough times, *I* want the option to feel sorry for myself and to get angry at Him. *I* want the option to withhold from Him my praise, my thanksgiving, my love, and my trust, because He's not treating me as nicely as *I* think He should." This is exactly what satan is hoping for and trying to do. If this becomes our attitude and our decision, then satan wins, we lose, and God greatly grieves over us.

Even if we are not angry, even if all we do is withhold our "Yes, God, I will trust You," that means we're still holding on to this ugly, selfish alternative to faith in God. I know it is not easy to trust God, especially at first, but He will prove Himself to be faithful to you.

LET'S ASK HIM:

> Yes, God, I want to believe Your Word. I want to believe what You say about Yourself.
>
> I want to reject everything that argues against Your holiness, Your absolute perfection and completeness.
>
> I want to totally depend upon You, and on You alone, especially in difficult times.
>
> Strengthen and deepen my faith in You, more and more, by Your Spirit within me.
>
> I ask You in the victory and authority of Jesus, Your Son.

CHAPTER SIX

THE LOVING GOD—FAR, FAR ABOVE ALL

Greatness Beyond Measure

Suppose for a moment that you had a friend who was full of love, grace, kindness, and generosity, someone who greatly desired to help you but who had no power or resources to act on it, and had no knowledge or wisdom to know how to do it properly. In spite of his lovely inner character and good loving intentions, he would be unable to help when you needed him.

So, before we take a closer look at the beautiful and lovely inner Heart of God, we are briefly going to look at the awesome external features of God's being, position, and power. We will see that He has infinite ability, power, and wisdom to always adequately express His loving nature and character to us in a multitude of beneficial ways. Nothing can stop Him, except our own refusal to receive Him and His great love.

I use the term *external* attributes to differentiate them from God's *internal* attributes—namely, His nature and character. Theologians label them "essential" and "moral" attributes, respectively. But I don't like to use these terms, because it infers that the "moral" attributes are not essential. His "essential" and "moral" attributes are all absolutely necessary (essential) to His holiness—His completeness. If any were missing in either of these categories, He would not be holy.

GOD'S BEING—WHO IN HEAVEN IS GOD?

God Is a Person

God is not a force, a cosmic power, or just an influence for good. He has all the characteristics of a person: self–consciousness, intelligence, free will, individual personality, emotions, and feelings. He is always referred to in Scripture as a person. He has personal names and performs personal acts. He has personal feelings. He can be pleased and delighted—or hurt and angered. He wants to be, and deserves to be, treated as a person—accepted, loved, talked to, listened to, answered, and trusted. He created us in His own image—and we turned out to be persons (like He is)—His own beloved children. I'm so glad He is a warm, loving Person who we can know and relate to, and not some cold, distant, impersonal force.

> Then God said, "Let Us make man in Our image, according to Our likeness"… So God created man in His own image; in the image of God He created him; male and female He created them. (Genesis 1:26–27)

God Is Eternal

God has always existed and always will. He has no beginning and no ending. He has infinite existence. This is beyond our limited comprehension. He is not limited or confined to time and space. He will always be here for us. We can count on Him. We can depend on Him, and be secure.

Even from everlasting to everlasting, You are God. (Psalm 90:2)

The everlasting God, the LORD, the Creator of the ends of the earth... (Isaiah 40:28)

The eternal God is your refuge, and underneath are the everlasting arms. (Deuteronomy 33:27)

God Is Unchanging

God does not, and cannot, change. He always remains the same. He is not fickle, unstable, erratic, or temperamental. All of Who He is remains eternally constant, holy, and perfect. He is true and faithful. We can always be confident that He remains steady, and we can put our unwavering trust in Him.

I am the LORD, I do not change. (Malachi 3:6)

Jesus Christ is the same yesterday, today, and forever. (Hebrews 13:8)

Every good gift and every perfect gift is from above, and comes down from the Father of lights, with whom there is no variation or shadow [hint] of turning [changing]. (James 1:17)

God Is Self-Existent

God is always self-sufficient and self-sustaining. He doesn't need to depend or rely on anyone or anything else. He has all sufficiency in all things. He has more than we shall ever need. He will never run short of anything. We can always trust that

He will provide for us.

> God, who made the world and everything in
> it, since He is Lord of heaven and earth, does
> not dwell in temples made with hands. Nor
> is He worshiped with men's hands, as though
> He needed anything, since He gives to all life,
> breath, and all things. (Acts 17:24–25)

God Is a Tri-Unity (Trinity)

Although God is One Person, He manifests Himself in three separate, distinct personal relationships. Each is an intimate love–relationship, and each is a family–relationship:

- God the Father, as our Heavenly *Father.*

- God the Son, as our *Brother, "became flesh
  [a man] and dwelt among us"* (John 1:14).

- God the Holy Spirit, as our spiritual *Husband*, unites with our spirits and we become the Bride of Christ (2 Corinthians 11:2; Hosea 2:19–20; 1 Corinthians 6:17; Revelation 19:7–8).

It's a wonderful mystery. How can God reveal Himself so differently and still be One? Well, He made us in His image: male and female, husband and wife, father and mother. He also made us His children (Genesis 1:26–28). In other words, God created family to be a mirror image of how He wants to lovingly relate with us on three different levels.

For example, a man at a family gathering can simultaneously interact as a son, a husband, and a father. In these three relationships, he will be relating very differently, and sometimes oppositely, but he is still the one man with the same nature and character. I believe God has so much love for us that He created three very different family/love–relationships in order to more fully express His wonderful love. God wants us to be in a close family/love–relationship with Him.

> For there are three that bear witness in heaven: the Father, the Word [the Son], and the Holy Spirit; and these three are one. (1 John 5:7)

> …Jesus [the Son] also was baptized; and while He prayed, the heaven was opened. And the Holy Spirit descended in bodily form like a dove upon Him, and a voice [the Father] came from heaven which said, "You are My beloved Son; in You I am well pleased." (Luke 3:21–22)

> And without controversy great is the mystery of godliness: God [the Father] was manifested in the flesh [the Son], justified in [authenticated by] the [Holy] Spirit… (1 Timothy 3:16)

God Is Glorious

God is full of magnificence, splendor, majesty, and awesome beauty. He created all the wonderful grandeur and exquisite beauty in the whole universe out of His own nature and glory. He is altogether marvelous in His resplendent brilliance and glorious excellence. He is more than worthy of all our awe, love, adoration, praise, and worship.

Be exalted, O God, above the heavens; let Your glory be above all the earth. (Psalm 57:5)

The heavens declare the glory of God; and the firmament [the expanse of sky] shows His handiwork. (Psalm 19:1)

For since the creation of the world His [God's] invisible attributes are clearly seen, being understood by the things that are made, even His eternal power and Godhead [divine nature]… (Romans 1:20)

O Lord my God, You are very great: You are clothed with honor and majesty. (Psalm 104:1)

Holy, holy, holy is the Lord of hosts; the whole earth is full of His glory! (Isaiah 6:3)

I will meditate on the glorious splendor of Your majesty, and on Your wondrous works. (Psalm 145:5)

God's Position—Who on Earth is God?

God Is Supreme

God is far above all else, always and absolutely incomparable. There is none higher or greater. He alone is the absolute ruler of the whole universe. Rightfully to Him, and to Him alone, belongs all our worship, reverence, submission, and obedience.

For the Lord your God is God of gods and Lord of lords, the great God, mighty and awesome... (Deuteronomy 10:17)

> Yours, O LORD, is the greatness, the power and
> the glory, the victory and the majesty; for all
> that is in heaven and in earth is Yours; Yours is
> the kingdom, O LORD, and You are exalted as
> head over all. (1 Chronicles 29:11)

God Is Sovereign

God is always the ultimate authority. He is answerable to no
one else. He is completely autonomous. He is transcendent
over all others. He has absolute reign over heaven and earth.
He is the only One with the right to rule over all that He has
created. It is only right that His will be done in our lives.

> Therefore know this day, and consider it in
> your heart, that the LORD Himself is God in
> heaven above and on the earth beneath; there
> is no other. (Deuteronomy 4:39)

> For the LORD is the great God, and the great
> King above all gods. (Psalm 95:3)

> But our God is in heaven; He does whatever He
> pleases. (Psalm 115:3)

God Is Unique

God is the only God. There is no other God in existence. He
is far above all other so-called "gods." All others are false, evil
impostors, and destructive deceivers. The Lord who created
the heavens and the earth is absolutely unequaled and unsur-

passed. He, and He alone, must be our God, our highest priority, our only and supreme Lord.

> Therefore know this day, and consider it in your heart, that the LORD Himself is God in heaven above and on the earth beneath; there is no other. (Deuteronomy 4:39)

> For I am God, and there is no other; I am God, and there is none like Me. (Isaiah 46:9)

> That they may know from the rising of the sun to its setting that there is none besides Me. I am the LORD, and there is no other. (Isaiah 45:6)

> You [Jesus] have spoken the truth, for there is one God, and there is no other but He. (Mark 12:32)

God Is the Creator

God created all the heavens and the earth, and everything that is in them. He created everything that is visible and invisible. There is nothing that exists that was not made by Him. From the tiniest subatomic particles to the greatest and farthest galaxies, He designed it all and brought it into being. He created us as His children, and gives us life and breath. It is only right to acknowledge His creatorship and joyfully embrace His rightful, supreme rule over us.

> In the beginning God created the heavens and the earth. (Genesis 1:1)

All things were made through Him, and without Him nothing was made that was made. (John 1:3)

For by Him all things were created that are in heaven and that are on earth, visible and invisible... All things were created through Him and for Him. (Colossians 1:16)

By faith we understand that the worlds were framed by the word of God, so that the things which are seen were not made of things which are visible. (Hebrews 11:3)

You are worthy, O Lord, to receive glory and honor and power; for You created all things, and by Your will they exist and were created. (Revelation 4:11)

God's Power—Can There Actually Be "Nothing Impossible"?

God Is Ever-Present

God's presence constantly fills the entire universe. He is always present everywhere at the same time. There is nowhere we can go where He is not present. This is beyond human comprehension. God is not limited in any way by time and space. He created them. He is there with us at all times and in all places.

...Behold, heaven and the heaven of heavens [the universe] cannot contain You [God]. (1 Kings 8:27)

"Can anyone hide himself in secret places, so I shall not see him?" says the Lord; "Do I not fill heaven and earth?" says the Lord. (Jeremiah 23:24)

Where can I go from Your Spirit? Or where can I flee from Your presence? If I ascend into heaven, You are there; if I make my bed in hell, behold, You are there. If I take the wings of the morning, and dwell in the uttermost parts of the sea, even there Your hand shall lead me, and Your right hand shall hold me. (Psalm 139:7–10)

God Is All-Powerful

God is always, and in every way, all–powerful. He has unlimited and universal power. He created, and still retains, all power and energy in the whole universe. He created all the laws of nature, and He can overrule them any time He wants to. He is the God of miracles. There is no task or person too difficult or impossible for Him. We can rejoice that nothing in us, or in our lives, is ever impossible to God.

…the Lord appeared to Abram and said to him, "I am Almighty God…" (Genesis 17:1)

…Alleluia! For the Lord God Omnipotent [all–powerful] reigns! (Revelation 19:6)

[Jesus said,] "with God all things are possible." (Matthew 19:26)

For with God nothing will be impossible.
(Luke 1:37)

[God] is able to do exceedingly abundantly
above all that we ask or think… (Ephesians
3:20)

God Has All Knowledge and Wisdom

God always knows everything about all things. He has infinite
knowledge. He perfectly knows all the past, the present, and
the future. Nothing can take Him by surprise. He has infinite
wisdom—the perfect ability to always use all His knowledge in
the best, right, and most advantageous way. He always knows
every detail of our lives, and exactly what is best for us. We can
utterly trust His knowledge and wisdom in every circumstance.

Great is our Lord, and mighty in power; His
understanding is infinite. (Psalm 147:5)

Oh, the depth of the riches both of the wisdom
and knowledge of God! How unsearchable are
His judgments and His ways past finding out!
(Romans 11:33)

"For My thoughts are not your thoughts, nor
are your ways My ways," says the LORD. "For
as the heavens are higher than the earth, so
are My ways higher than your ways, and My
thoughts than your thoughts." (Isaiah 55:8–9)

[Christ] in whom are hidden all the treasures
of wisdom and knowledge. (Colossians 2:3)

What an awesome God! The eternal, unchangeable, supreme, sovereign, all–powerful, all–wise, and always–present Creator is *far beyond* the limits of our human comprehension. I'm glad that He is far beyond the very limited extent of my intellect and the puny scope of my logic. If He wasn't much, much greater than what I can comprehend, He wouldn't be much of a God. But He abundantly has *all* the capabilities, power, and authority to *always* fully express to us His truly wonderful inner nature and His great, good, loving Heart.

LET'S ASK HIM:

> Oh, God! You are more than I can comprehend. Please give me the faith to believe what You say in Your Word about Yourself.

> Fill me with true awe and wonder as to all that You really are.

> Help me to have the right attitude of submission to Your supreme sovereignty as my Creator and my Maker.

> Enable me to confidently trust in Your power and Your wisdom.

> I ask this in all the love and authority of Jesus' name.

PART TWO

God's Real Inner Heart and Nature

CHAPTER SEVEN

GOD IS POWERFUL—BUT IS HE REALLY GOOD?

God's Wonderful Inner Heart for Us

THE BIG BURNING QUESTION

As wonderful and awesome as these external attributes of God are, they tell us nothing of His inner nature, His character, or His temperament. He is all-powerful and all-wise, but what kind of a person is He like inside? He is sovereign and supreme, but what are His real Heart and His personality like? He is eternal and unchanging, but what are His inner qualities, and what is His true disposition?

Is God kind or cruel? Is He tender-hearted or hard-hearted? Is He forgiving and full of grace or is He unforgiving and full of revenge? Is He kind and compassionate or stern and harsh? Is He longsuffering or quick-tempered and irritable? Will He always tell us the truth and be good to us or will He sometimes trick us, manipulate us, or violate us? Will He be kind and generous or stingy and miserly?

It is of the utmost importance that we find out what the inner Heart of our Creator, our God, is truly like. It will mean the difference between trusting Him or being afraid of Him, between believing Him or doubting Him, wanting Him or rejecting Him, and loving Him or hating Him.

DOES GOD ACTUALLY HAVE TWO SIDES?

Yes, there do seem to be two sides to God's goodness. We began to see this in Chapter 2, in what God proclaimed to Moses on Mount Sinai (Exodus 34:5–7):

- Love: On the one side, there is mercy, tenderness, grace, patience, and forgiveness.

- Justice: On the other side, there is truth, faithfulness, righteousness, and judgment.

At times, these two different aspects of God's nature seem to be contrary to each other, but no, they are very definitely not in conflict. They are marvelously and inextricably harmonized. These two facets of God's character are always fully expressed and always blended together, and they make a beautiful and amazingly whole, perfect Person.

TWO BAD SCENES

Let me illustrate my point. Suppose you had someone treat you with wonderful, kind, compassionate, tender love, but in the end it proved to be false, just a pretense. The person was so sweet and promised lovely things to you, but it was all a lie. You were deceived and used. It was all a con job. Wouldn't you be deeply hurt and terribly disappointed? No matter how nice it seemed for a while, it would be a very bad scene, because it would be *Love—without Truth.*

But, on the other hand, suppose someone dealt with you in only hard, cold truth about all your faults, without any love, tenderness, mercy, grace, or forgiveness. They gave you the whole, cutting, searing truth about your shortcomings, with no softness or kindness. With no patience or tolerance, they fully gave you what you deserved for everything you did wrong—you only got cold justice. Everything was harsh and strict, with no patience or leniency. Wouldn't you be hurt again and again? This too would be a very bad scene, because it would be *Truth—without Love.*

THE VERY BEST SCENE POSSIBLE

But suppose someone poured out extravagant love, affection, tender kindness, care, and consideration upon you. They cherished you and proved how precious you are to them by words and deeds. With utmost kindness, grace and generosity, they treated you very patiently. They extended total forgiveness every time you did something wrong. They always strived for your highest good. Their patience, mercy, and forgiveness covered all your wrongs. And they consistently did all this in absolute truth, faithfulness, integrity, and righteousness. It was all sincere and without any ulterior motive. It was all true! This is the very best scene possible. This is *Love—combined with Truth*—or, in other words, *True Love.*

Truth without love can be brutality. Love without truth can be deception. But when truth and love are combined it is a beautiful and glorious reality. God, our perfect Creator and loving Father, is absolute, infinite, unfailing true love—beyond measure.

Do you see how these two aspects (sides) of God's real nature, Love and Truth, must always be perfectly united and blended together? He is not just one or the other. He is both at the same time, all the time. God is perfect, complete, and holy. He does not swing back and forth from one to the other. That is the mark of an unstable person. God is not a split–personality. God will *always* completely fulfill and express both of these two facets of His beautiful and perfect goodness. There is more about this in Chapter 13.

THE BIG BLAZING ANSWER

In many ways, and many times, throughout Scripture, these two aspects (sides) of God are seen together in perfect integration and harmony. They both are succinctly expressed in the book of 1 John:

> This is the message which we have heard from Him [Jesus] and declare to you, that God is light and in Him is no darkness at all. (1 John 1:5)

"Light," as used here, is a metaphor for truth, faithfulness, righteousness, and justice. We will explore this in Chapters 10 and 11.

> …God is love. In this the love of God was manifested toward us, that God has sent His only begotten Son into the world, that we might live through Him. (1 John 4:8–9)

> And we have known and believed the love that God has for us. God is love… (1 John 4:16)

"Love," in these verses, is translated from the Greek word *agape*, which is a special kind of love which means "the love of God." It is not human love, but divine love. It is far above and beyond human love and every human effort to achieve it. We will explore this *agape* love in the next two chapters.

Light and love. This is what God *is*—not just what He has, what He does, or what He gives, but what He *is*—in the core and essence of His Being. This is His nature and His real Heart. He is always both light and love perfectly combined. Both are perfectly balanced, and they supplement and complement each other, making God a beautiful, whole, complete, and perfect God. *"Holy, holy, holy"* (Isaiah 6:3). Astounding True Love!

LET'S ASK HIM:

> God, I want to see deep into Your real Heart and nature. Please, show me what You are at the very core of Your Being.
>
> Enable me to trust You and love You more and more.
>
> Give me understanding of how Your love and Your light always work together.
>
> Jesus, open the eyes of my spirit and reveal to me the Father's great, true love.
>
> I ask this in the supreme authority and power of Your name.

CHAPTER EIGHT

TRUE LOVE—FAR, FAR ABOVE ALL LOVE

Astounding Love, Beyond Measure

THE REAL CORE OF GOD'S PERFECT HEART

One of the greatest statements in Scripture is *"God is love."*

He who does not love does not know God, for God is love... And we have known [experienced] and believed the love that God has for us. God is love, and he who abides in love abides in God, and God in him. (1 John 4:8, 16)

Twice in this one chapter, the Spirit of God says that love is Who God is—not just what He has, what He gives, or what He does, but Who He *is*—at the very center of His Being.

God is perfect love. I deliberately use the word "perfect," because the Scriptures make it very clear that God is holy (see Chapter 5). "Holy" means whole, complete, entire, and absolute perfection. Everything about God is complete and perfect. So God is *infinite, eternal, perfect, true love.*

I have carefully studied my way through the Scriptures many times and have come to see that love is the main characteristic of God's inner nature and real Heart. It is not the only part of His character, but it is certainly the main one. How wonderful this is for us, because though we are self-willed, straying, sinning humans, we are still the object and focus of His great true love.

The New Testament Scriptures were originally written in the Greek language, and the Greeks had four different words for "love," whereas we only have one word in English. They had one word for family–love, another for friendship–love, another for romantic–love, and another special word for God–love.

The Greek word for God–love is *agape*, and this is the word used above in 1 John 4:8, 16. Although the other kinds of love came from God when He created us as His children, *agape* love is the special kind of love that only God has. To differentiate this special God–love from human–love, I will begin using the term "*agape* love."

Agape love is not human love as are the other types of love. It is much higher. We do not naturally have *agape* love in us, nor can we produce it ourselves. But we can receive it from God as a gift, then lovingly express it back to Him. We can also pass it on to other people around us. It is unique, and only God can give it. And He gives it only by His Holy Spirit:

> Now hope does not disappoint, because the [*agape*] love of God has been poured out in our hearts by the Holy Spirit who was given to us. (Romans 5:5)

> But the fruit of the Spirit is [*agape*] love… (Galatians 5:22)

...that you, being rooted and grounded in
[*agape*] love, may be able to comprehend with
all the saints [believers] what is the width and
length and depth and height—to know [expe-
rience] the [*agape*] love of Christ which passes
knowledge; that you may be filled with all the
fullness of God. (Ephesians 3:17–19)

God eagerly wants us to experience His *agape* love, even
though it goes far beyond the reaches of human comprehension and is exceedingly fervent, vast, and multifaceted. He
wants His children to increasingly experience and enjoy His
great, passionate *agape* love as much as is humanly possible.
The main characteristics of God's *agape* love are made very
clear, again and again, in His Scriptures.

THE MAIN CHARACTERISTICS OF
GOD'S GREAT *AGAPE* LOVE

God Intensely Desires a Loving Father/Child
Relationship with Each of Us

It is impossible to fully comprehend how greatly and intensely
God desires a close, loving relationship with us, His children.
He passionately yearns for us to be reconciled back to Himself
and to be close to Him again. In the beginning, He created us
to be His children (Genesis 1:27), and even before the foundation of the world He chose each one of us (Ephesians 1:4), because He fervently wanted a multitude of children upon whom
He could lavishly pour out His great and wonderful *agape* love.

How much does God yearn for us, His children, and fervently want us back in His arms again? Even though we all have sinned, have gone astray, gone our own selfish way, and are not at all worthy, God still greatly, deeply, and passionately desires this close, loving, family–relationship with us. What an extremely high value He places on this relationship!

See how greatly and intensely God wants us all back in His wonderful loving arms of true love. Look at the incredible price He paid for each of us to be forgiven and reconciled back to Him. Read the thirty statements below and begin to see how intensely He loves and desires every one of us fallen sinning children.

The High Price God Paid to Win Us Back to Himself

God, Who is Spirit,
  manifested Himself to us in human flesh.
  (John 4:24; 1 Timothy 3:16)

God, The Word,
  expressing His love, became
  flesh and dwelt among us.
  (John 1:1–4, 14)

The Invisible God
  revealed Himself to us in a visible image.
  (Colossians 1:15)

The Most High God
  made Himself lower than the angels.
  (Deuteronomy 10:17; Hebrews 2:9–10)

The Great Creator
  stepped down and became just like us.
  (Genesis 1:1; Hebrews 2:14–15)

THE ETERNAL GOD
stepped into the confines of time and space.
(Isaiah 57:15; Luke 2:7)

GOD THE FATHER
sent His own Son in the likeness
of sinful flesh, and for sin.
(Romans 8:3)

THE BRIGHTNESS OF GOD'S GLORY
was born of a virgin.
(Hebrews 1:3; Isaiah 7:14; Galatians 4:4)

THE GOD WHO IS EVERYWHERE
confined Himself to a human body.
(1 Kings 8:27; Luke 2:11–12)

THE ALL-POWERFUL GOD
became a helpless newborn baby.
(Genesis 17:1; Luke 2:7)

THE HEAVENLY FATHER
named His Son Jesus [God saves],
"Son of the Highest."
(Luke 1:30–32)

THE ALMIGHTY GOD
also called His name "Immanuel"
[God with us].
(Genesis 17:1; Isaiah 7:14)

THE MAJESTY ON HIGH
commanded all the angels to
worship "the firstborn."
(Hebrews 1:3, 6)

The All-Wise God,
    as a child, needed to be taught and to learn.
       (Psalm 147:5; Romans 16:27; Luke 2:46)

The Unchanging God,
    as a child, had to develop, grow, and mature.
       (Malachi 3:6; Luke 2:52)

The Father of Glory
    came with no stately form, splendor, or beauty.
       (Ephesians 1:17; Isaiah 53:2)

The Lord of Lords
    took the form of a servant, just like men.
       (Deuteronomy 10:17; Philippians 2:7)

The Father of Lights
    put all His fullness, bodily, in Jesus.
       (James 1:17; Colossians 1:19, 2:9)

The Holy Father
    made Jesus the brightness and
    express image of His person.
       (Hebrews 1:1–3)

The King of All Kings
    submitted Himself to earthly authorities.
       (Revelation 19:16; Luke 2:51)

The Maker of Heaven and Earth
    laid aside His glory, became poor.
       (John 1:3; 2 Corinthians 8:9)

The Supreme Ruler of All
    descended to be a lowly peasant carpenter.
       (Daniel 4:17; Mark 6:3)

THE SOVEREIGN GOD
became a servant and learned obedience.
(Psalm 95:3; Hebrews 5:8)

THE FATHER OF GLORY
was despised, mocked, and suffered shame.
(Ephesians 1:17; Isaiah 53:3; Hebrews 12:2)

THE GOD ABOVE ALL
greatly humbled Himself.
(Deuteronomy 10:17; Philippians 2:5–8)

THE LIVING GOD
took our sin and our death upon Himself.
(Psalm 42:2; Isaiah 53:5–6; 1 Peter 2:24, 3:18)

THE HOLY, HOLY, HOLY GOD
became sin for us.
(Isaiah 6:3; Revelation 4:8; 2 Corinthians 5:21)

THE GOD IN THE HIGHEST HEAVEN
paid for our sin in the lowest hell.
(Luke 2:14; Acts 2:31)

THE GOD WHO IS LOVE WAS IN CHRIST,
reconciling the world to Himself.
(John 3:16; 2 Corinthians 5:19)

THE GOD OF LIFE
raised up Jesus and exalted Him far above all.
(Ephesians 1:19–23; Philippians 2:6–11)

Why? Why did God do all of this for us? Why pay such a great price? Because He *agape* loves us so greatly and longs for us so intensely. We are so incredibly precious to Him. He loves us—more than we can possibly imagine.

It is utterly astounding! So totally amazing! Beyond our comprehension! Yet it is within our grasp to at least begin to know, receive, and enjoy this incredible, intense *agape* love of God.

> For God so [*agape*] loved the world [you, me, and every other human being] that He gave His only begotten Son [Jesus], that whoever believes in Him should not perish but have everlasting life. (John 3:16)

Take the time to read the accounts of Jesus' betrayal, crucifixion and resurrection in these chapters: Matthew 26–28, Mark 14–16, Luke 22–24, and John 18–20.

See for yourself how much suffering, pain, agony, humiliation, reviling, and rejection Jesus willingly went through, at the insistence of God the Father, because our loving Father so intensely desires to have us back, embrace us in His arms of love, and enjoy us as His children. Take a look at Chapter 19 and see Him lovingly embrace us in His great, big arms.

Jesus loves us more than all the glories of Heaven—He laid them aside. He loves us more than He hates our sin—He took our sin upon Himself on that cross. He loves us more than He loved Himself—He sacrificed Himself for us. How greatly the Father and the Son want us and yearn for you and me and every person on Earth. Believe it. It's astounding true love—beyond measure.

But think of the agony the Father Himself had in His great Heart of love when He planned all the painful details of His Beloved Son's betrayal and crucifixion and when He prophesied it in His Word hundreds of years beforehand. How His Heart must have been torn to shreds when Jesus pleaded with Him three times in the garden of Gethsemane (Matthew

26:36–44), with *"vehement cries and tears"* (Hebrews 5:7) and *"sweat... like great drops of blood"* (Luke 22:44), *"O My Father, if it is possible, let this cup pass from Me; nevertheless, not as I will, but as You will"* (Matthew 26:39).

But the Father loved us so passionately and so intensely that He asked His Only Beloved Son, Jesus, to go through all the horrible suffering—the beatings, the whipping, the carrying of the cross, the crown of thorns, the nails driven into His hands and feet, and the six long torturous hours of crucifixion. Then, for three days and nights, His soul suffered the horrors of the depths of hell, taking on Himself our sin, our guilt, and our condemnation.

"And the LORD *has laid on Him [Jesus] the iniquity of us all... [The* LORD *made] His soul an offering for sin"* (Isaiah 53:6, 10). *"For He [God] made Him [Jesus] who knew no sin to be sin for us"* (2 Corinthians 5:21). That is why, at the end of the six hours on the cross, Jesus screamed, *"My God, My God, why have You forsaken Me?"* (Matthew 27:46). God had to turn away from His own beloved Son and deliver His soul to the depths of hell. How painful all this must have also been for the Father. How deep must have been the agony and anguish in His great Father's Heart. God the Father *"was in Christ, reconciling the world to Himself"* (2 Corinthians 5:19). The Father Himself was suffering incredibly for us, through Jesus. The intensity of His great, pure, loving desire for us is far, far beyond our human comprehension.

An Illustration: Your Own Lost Child

Suppose you are a very loving father or mother. Imagine you are out camping and your precious little child wanders away into the forest and becomes lost. Do you just sit comfortably by the campfire and calmly wish that your precious child somehow makes it back to you? No! Wouldn't you leave that warm, cheery campfire and go out into the dark, cold forest, crying, calling, yearning, longing, praying, searching, doing all you can, even being willing to die, to rescue your precious little one? God has done so much more than all that for us, His little children.

God's *agape* love is far greater than the love of any earthly parent. We are lost without Him. God has done, is now doing, and will continue to do, all He can to rescue us from our state of lostness. Can you now understand a little of how intensely He desires and longs for us, His dear, precious children and why He so eagerly paid such an incredible price to get us back?

God completely loves and will continue to love, *equally*, every person in all of human history, knowing very well that many will never receive Him or ever love Him back in return. But He will love them anyway, because this is His nature, His character. This is His real Heart. It is truly the ultimate, infinite sacrificial true love. He loves the whole world and desires everyone to come to Him, regardless of how good or bad, rich or poor they are; regardless of race, ethnicity, gender, religion, or degree of sinfulness. He intensely desires this close, warm, loving Father–relationship with us all. This is Who He is. He will never change. He *agape* loves us totally, passionately, equally, and eternally because He is absolute, true love.

God Intensely Delights in Us

The word "delight" is a strong word. It means great pleasure, extreme enjoyment, intense and joyful satisfaction. That is what God feels towards you and me when we turn back to Him and let ourselves be found by Him. Don't let satan whisper to you that God may feel that way about others, but not about you. God, through Jesus, died for you, intensely desires you, and intensely delights in you as much as any other person on earth.

How much does God delight in us? Let's continue on with the above illustration. Suppose you have been charging through the dark, cold forest for a long time, weeping, calling desperately, shouting at the top of your voice, searching anxiously for your precious child, and suddenly you find the one you love!

Will you be angry and upset because of all the worry they have caused you? Will you scold, berate, and punish your priceless little one? Will you reject the one you created? Wouldn't you instead hug them, kiss them, hold them very close, and tell them how glad you are that they're safe and how much you love them? Wouldn't you cry for joy, greatly celebrating and delighting in your darling little child even though he or she is dirty, scratched, muddy, tear-stained, and disheveled? And even though he or she had disobeyed you and wandered away, causing you so much anguish, anxiety, and pain, wouldn't you freely and joyfully forgive them?

Jesus told a story about this very thing in Luke 15:3–7. A shepherd loses one sheep out of his flock of one hundred. He leaves the ninety-nine and goes after the one which is lost.

When he finds it, he carries it on his shoulders, rejoicing. He calls all his friends and neighbors and says, *"Rejoice with me, for I have found my sheep which was lost"* (Luke 15:6). Then Jesus said to the people, *"likewise there will be more joy in heaven over one sinner who repents than over ninety-nine just persons who need no repentance"* (Luke 15:7). The shepherd surely loved all His sheep equally, but His *special* rejoicing over a lost one who has been found is because of the tragedy that had been averted. So it is with God and us, His children.

Before God began to show me His true Heart and His great *agape* love, I had this very wrong picture in my mind: "God is absolutely holy and hates sin. But because of His compassion, He reached down to me, so imperfect and so sinful. And because He hates sin, He held His nose, turned His head away, picked me up, gritted His teeth, held me at arm's length, and started dragging me to heaven, reluctantly enduring my failings, my faults, and my sins with great displeasure."

Nothing could be farther from the truth. It was all a lie and a slander from the enemy. I believed it because I didn't know the greatness of His true *agape* love—His wonderful Heart. I had great difficulty believing that He could actually have any great pleasure or extreme enjoyment in an imperfect, stumbling person like me.

At the very moment we turn back to God (repent), and receive (by faith) His great *agape* love through Jesus' death and resurrection, He joyfully forgives us, washes us clean, puts His Spirit in us, changes us on the inside, and clothes us with Jesus' perfect righteousness. And He does all this because He loves us and delights in us. We are not repulsive to Him. He delights in cleansing us and clothing us with His righteousness. We are still imperfect, but we are forgiven and washed clean by Jesus' blood. The Father now sees us as righteous! He was very willing to pay that immense price for us, His children.

Hebrews 12:2 says, *"for the joy that was set before Him [Jesus] endured the cross, despising the shame."* What was the *"joy set before Him"*? It was you and me, and all who will turn their hearts back to Him, give themselves to Him, receive and love Him. His Father–desire for us, and His Father–delight in us, were greater than all the pain, shame, death, and hell of His cross.

Isaiah 53:10–11 says, *"He shall see His seed [His children]… He shall see the labor [travail] of His soul, and be satisfied."* What made *"the labor of His soul"* so satisfying? It was you and me, and all His reconciled children, now enjoying Him and loving Him in return. We are worth more to Him than all His suffering, shame, and travail.

But how can this be? We are so sinful and foolish. We mess things up so badly and so often. We have caused Him so much pain. How can we failing humans be worth that much to Him?

Another Illustration: Your Own Baby

Imagine a husband and wife whose home is clean, neat, and tidy and whose life is peaceful and orderly. Their nights are calm, quiet, and undisturbed. Eventually they have a much longed–for baby, their own precious, cherished child. They bring it home, and suddenly their peace and quiet is gone. Their nights are very disturbed. The orderliness is upset and their schedules are scrambled. They now have to deal with wet and smelly diapers, crying and wailing, loss of sleep, extra expenses, and many more demands on their time.

Are these parents now disillusioned and disgruntled? Do they hate their baby? No, a thousand times no! In spite of all that their baby does, or does not do, they pour out their love, affection, and adoration upon it. They intensely longed for it, and now they greatly delight in their very own little child. Regardless of all the dirty messes, the "throwing up" on their shoulders, the lost sleep, the extra expenses, the inconveniences and the sacrifices they must make, they passionately delight in their little one. They receive much pleasure, great joy, and deep satisfaction from him or her, simply because it is their own child. This helpless little baby doesn't have to do anything to earn or deserve its parents' great love and delight. It gets all that love just because it was born into their family.

God, speaking through the prophet Zephaniah, says to us, *"The LORD your God in your midst, the Mighty One, will save; He will rejoice over you with gladness, He will quiet you with His love, He will rejoice over you with singing"* (Zephaniah 3:17). This gives me a picture of a loving mother, quieting and soothing her hurting child in her arms, and singing a lullaby to it. Believe what God says to us. It's true! Don't believe the devil's lies. God delights in you and me this way, and even much, much more than we can imagine.

When a child gets older, he or she may disappoint, hurt, or anger their parents or even break their parents' hearts, but if they are good loving parents they will continue to love their child who will still be the treasure of their heart and the object of their love and intense desire. How *much more* loving is God, the perfect and merciful Father, toward us!

You see, when we turn to God with all our heart, and by

faith receive Jesus and all He did for us on the cross, and we sincerely give ourselves back to Him and to His Lordship, He, by His Spirit, comes into us, unites with our spirit, and we are spiritually born into God's family (John 3:3–8). Immediately, the blood that Jesus shed for us on the cross washes away all our sin, guilt, and condemnation (past, present, and future), and then God embraces us, enjoys us, and delights in us, even though we are still far from perfect. But up until the point when we turn our heart to Him and receive Him and His love, God has been intensely longing and yearning for us, calling to us with an aching, unsatisfied, and broken Heart. God's great *agape* love is immensely above and beyond the love of any earthly parent.

God Determines to Always Act for Our Highest Good

As God's *agape* love is the very core of His real nature, so this third main aspect is the very core of His *agape* love. God's love for us is *not* just nice desires, emotions, and feelings. It is also action—practical action. He has *not* just stayed away up in Heaven having nice thoughts about us; He has come down to earth to take action and to always work for our highest possible benefit, at great pain and sacrifice to Himself. Remember, God became flesh (Jesus), took the form of a servant, came in the likeness of men, and became obedient—to the death of the cross (Philippians 2:5–8).

This aspect of His *agape* love is not just a wish that God has for us. It is an intense, strong determination to always work for our greatest benefit. Determination is even stronger than desire. He has determined to implement this desire, no matter what. This is as sure as God is sure. He is absolutely faithful.

He is totally for us—not against us. He loves us. We are His children. He wants the best for us. He will always work toward our highest good, because He is love—true love, beyond measure!

> If God is for us, who can be against us? He who did not spare His own Son [Jesus], but delivered Him up [to death] for us all, how shall He not with Him also freely give us all things? (Romans 8:31–32)

> For I know the thoughts that I think toward you, says the LORD, thoughts of peace and not of evil [harm], to give you a future and a hope. (Jeremiah 29:11)

His intense determination is first and foremost for our eternal, heavenly good, and secondarily for our temporal, earthly good. He knows that our eternal benefit is always far more important than the earthly. So therefore, He will always keep that as His top priority, while working to give us His best right here and now, on earth.

His intense determination to always work for our greatest eternal good includes a desire to bestow upon us some good and beneficial pleasure here and now. He is not just a utilitarian taskmaster, using us as slaves to accomplish His purposes here on earth. God is our great loving Father and we are His small children. He is the One who created beauty and pleasure, good fun and enjoyment. Just look at creation all around us. Look at how we are made to enjoy things. God, like any good father, enjoys seeing His children enjoying themselves—and enjoying Him.

Manmade religion is usually demanding, cold, austere, harsh, and joyless. But an authentic relationship with God, and with Jesus, is not that way. He is good, *good*, **good**—far beyond measure!

But our earthly pleasures are only of secondary importance. God's main priority is to develop Christ's character in us (Romans 8:29). God loves us too much to spoil us by giving us everything that, in our childish foolishness, we ask for. Nor will He give us anything that would harm us or detract from our highest eternal good. Even natural parents, if they are wise, out of their love will sometimes say "No," for their children's own good. Don't be upset if God does not answer some prayers. He still loves you, but His thoughts and ways are much, much higher than ours (Isaiah 55:8–9) and are always for our highest eternal good.

God has promised in His word *"that all things work together for good to those who love God, to those who are the called according to His purpose"* (Romans 8:28). Now, when He says "all things," He means "all things." This is amazing! God, in His infinite love, wisdom, and power, will even take what wrong we do, or what wrong others do to us—even what evil things satan does to us—and work it together, along with His own workings, to eventually make good come out of it for us and for Him, and possibly for others also. What a wonderful, wise, and loving God He is!

God's *agape* love is completely unselfish, always sacrificing for us, and says, "Your benefit—at My expense." The opposite of *agape* love is self–love, which is selfishness, self–centeredness, self–interest, and self–serving. Selfishness says, "My benefit—at your expense." God is the exact opposite of selfishness. He sacrificed His own Son for us, for our highest eternal benefit—at His great expense—on that cruel, cruel cross.

God Intensely Desires Us to Love Him in Return

Jesus taught that the highest commandment God has ever given to the human race is: *"love [agape] the Lord your God with all your heart, with all your soul, with all your mind, and with all your strength"* (Mark 12:30). In other words, love Him completely and passionately. When we receive God's *agape* love through Jesus, He breathes His Spirit into our spirit, and then we have God's *agape* love within us. He greatly longs for us to love Him in return with this unselfish God–given love. He has commanded this, because He wants our love to be joyfully poured out back to Him.

> We [*agape*] love Him because He first [*agape*]
> loved us. (1 John 4:19)

Even though it is a command, He will not force us. He yearns for us to willingly obey this highest command with our own free will. Love must be willingly given. This is an inherent fact about love. Real love will not violate our free will. The moment love is demanded, compelled, or forced, it ceases to be love. The delight is gone. The control, manipulation, or force imposed produces an unwilling response. This is a form of emotional rape. Love then dies and becomes slavery and bondage.

I believe this is why God, in His wisdom, did not lock up satan when he first sinned against God many ages ago. And this is why God provided an option, a choice, for mankind in the garden of Eden, and why God allowed satan to come in and test Adam and Eve (see Genesis 2:16–17, 3:1–6). God could have put a very high fence around the Tree of the Knowledge of Good and Evil and put a very strong angel to guard it. He easily could have stopped satan from ever tempting the human race.

If He had done that, then we would have been locked–in robots, slaves without a choice. Our free–will love is so precious to God that He gave us an alternative, a choice—and He still does, every day. He doesn't force us to love Him, but instead gives us the awesome privilege to receive His great *agape* love and freely *agape* love Him in return. We were created for this. God wanted love–children. There is no greater joy and satisfaction, either for Him or for us.

Now, this is not selfishness on God's part. He did not *agape* love us with an ulterior, selfish motive. This is not His trade–off, saying, "I will love you *if* you love Me." God's love for us is completely unconditional, but He does deeply desire for us to love Him in return.

> But God demonstrates His own [*agape*] love toward us, in that while we were still sinners, Christ died for us… For if when we were enemies we were reconciled to God through the death of His Son, much more, having been reconciled, we shall be saved by His life. (Romans 5:8, 10)

> In this is [agape] love, not that we loved God,
> but that He [agape] loved us and sent His Son
> to be the propitiation [payment] for our sins...
> We [agape] love Him because He first [agape]
> loved us. (1 John 4:10, 19)

God loves every person whether or not they will ever love Him. But oh how He longs for us all to receive His great love and then willingly love Him in return. It is a great eternal fact about God's *agape love* that the God who delights to love us, also delights in being loved by us. He created love to be that way. He intensely enjoys it when we pour out our love back to Him.

This is what worship is all about—passionate, fervent love. "Worship" is defined as giving God highest honor, extravagant love, and total submission. In Scripture, God many times calls for our love and worship, but He will not force us. He will work patiently to win and woo us to Himself, but He will never force us, for He knows that would kill love. He will not violate the free will He so lovingly gave us. He deeply desires to have children who will freely and gladly pour out their love back to Him in return, thus delighting His great, loving Heart.

God Intensely Yearns for Our Love to Him to be Total and Joyful

Jesus did not say that the highest command was just to love God, but to *"love [agape] the Lord your God with all your heart, with all your soul, with all your mind, and with all your strength"* (Mark 12:30). Our love and worship for God must be wholehearted, sincere, total, and "full throttle" in order to satisfy and thrill His great Heart of love.

Partial or half-hearted love and weak worship is disobeying God's highest command. Apathetic, complacent, half-hearted, lukewarm worship is an insult to the great loving God, Creator of heaven and earth. It grieves His Heart and disappoints His highest desire and delight.

Jesus rebuked His church in Revelation 3:15–16 for being "lukewarm." He said, *"I know your works, that you are neither cold nor hot. I could wish you were cold or hot. So then, because you are lukewarm, and neither cold nor hot, I will vomit you out of My mouth."* It made Him sick. Half-hearted love and worship is the worst advertisement about God and about Jesus that we could ever give to the world around us. It says to the world that He is not wonderful, not awesome, not glorious, not the Greatest. It greatly dishonors Him.

But how thrilling it is to God when we love Him totally, passionately, and unconditionally! We are then delighting and pleasing the very center of His passionate Heart. *"He shall see the labor [travail] of His soul, and be satisfied"* (Isaiah 53:11). This was *"the joy that was set before Him"* (Hebrews 12:2) while dying on that cruel, cruel cross.

In the book of Psalms, God calls out to us again and again to give Him joyful worship more than He asks for any other attitude of worship. This reflects the desire of His real Heart. Because of how incredibly good and loving God is to us, anything less than joyful, wholehearted worship is being ungrateful and is displeasing, disappointing, and dishonoring to Him.

But let the righteous be glad; let them rejoice before God; yes, let them rejoice exceedingly. (Psalm 68:3)

> Rejoice in the Lord always. Again I will say, re-
> joice! (Philippians 4:4)

God's Agape Love Is Unending

God loved us long before we were born. He loves us now, and He will never cease loving us. His love is eternal. This is the very core of His nature. And His gift for us is eternal life, through Jesus Christ our Lord (Romans 6:23). This is His true love for us—beyond measure!

> Yes, I have loved you with an everlasting love;
> therefore with lovingkindness I have drawn
> you. (Jeremiah 31:3)

God's Agape Love Is Unlimited

God's love is so immense that it surpasses human knowledge. We will never get to the end of it, but He wants us to begin comprehending it and experiencing it as much as possible, right now.

> ...[That we] may be able to comprehend with
> all the saints [believers] what is the width and
> length and depth and height—to know [expe-
> rience] the [agape] love of Christ [God's love
> through Jesus] which passes knowledge...
> (Ephesians 3:18–19)

God's Agape Love Is Unconditional

God's love is a free gift. We cannot earn it, be worthy of it, or ever repay it. It is neither a loan nor a mortgage that we have to pay back for the rest of our lives. It is ours because He created us to be His love-children, so that He could lavish His love upon us. His love for us is always by His great grace, and grace is His free, undeserved favor. It is always a gift.

> But God demonstrates His own [agape] love toward us, in that while we were still sinners, Christ died for us… when we were [His] enemies we were reconciled to God through the death of His Son… (Romans 5:8, 10)

> For by grace you have been saved through faith, and that not of yourselves; it is the gift of God, not of works, lest anyone should boast. (Ephesians 2:8–9)

Here is another illustration. Suppose some loving parents, with great excitement, gave their son a very wonderful and precious gift for Christmas, and the son was so thrilled with it that he said to them, "This is a wonderful and costly gift, therefore I will work very hard and make monthly payments to you until I have paid you back completely." Wouldn't that take all the joy out of it for the parents? He has spoiled the whole idea of it being a love-gift. They would say, "No, this is a free love-gift. We give it because you are our son and we love you. Your gratitude and love alone will thrill and satisfy our hearts."

I have heard it said this way, "We can do nothing to make God love us *more*, and we can do nothing to make Him love us *less*." He already loves us totally, and no matter what we do, or do not do, He will keep on loving us totally, because God is love. But we can give Him great delight and pleasure—or we can cause Him disappointment, grief, and pain by ignoring, neglecting, or rejecting His great love. That can't change His Heart or change His love. But neglecting or rejecting God's love will result in a tragic, immense, and eternal loss for us— and great sorrow for Him.

God's Agape Love Is Unconquerable

Nothing can separate us from God's great love except our own stubborn rejection of Him and His love. It would be only our own choice, certainly not His.

> For I am convinced that neither death, nor life, nor angels, nor principalities, nor things present, nor things to come, nor powers, nor height, nor depth, nor any other created thing, will be able to separate us from the [agape] love of God which is in Christ Jesus our Lord. (Romans 8:38–39, NASB)

Only our own continued, stubborn rejection of Him, or simply ignoring or neglecting to receive Him, can separate us eternally from God's great love. Nothing else can.

God's Agape Love Is Unfailing

God is holy. And "holy" means that every part of His being and His character and nature is absolutely whole, complete, entire, total, infinite, eternal, and perfect (see Chapter 5). Therefore His love is whole, complete, and infinitely perfect. It cannot be anything less. His love cannot fail. We may fail, but He cannot. He is *agape* love to the very center of His being!

[*Agape*] Love never fails. (1 Corinthians 13:8)

If we are faithless, He remains faithful; He cannot deny Himself. (2 Timothy 2:13)

God's Agape Love Can Be Believed, Received, and Experienced

God's love is for every person, and it is waiting to be received and experienced. Receiving is a definite act of our will, and a step of faith. God is wanting, asking, and waiting for us to take that step.

> For God so [*agape*] loved the world that He gave His only begotten Son [Jesus], that whoever believes in Him should not perish but have everlasting life. For God did not send His Son into the world to condemn the world, but that the world through Him might be saved. (John 3:16–17)

> In this the [*agape*] love of God was manifested toward us, that God has sent His only begotten Son [Jesus] into the world, that we might live [eternally] through Him. (1 John 4:9)

> But as many as received Him [Jesus], to them He gave the right to become children of God, to those who believe in His name: who were born, not of blood, nor of the will of the flesh, nor of the will of man, but of God. (John 1:12–13)

> And we have known [experienced] and believed the [agape] love that God has for us. God is [agape] love, and he who abides in love abides in God, and God in him. (1 John 4:16)

Will you believe His love and, by simple child–like faith, receive Him? Will you receive His Son Jesus as your Savior and Lord? This is the only way we can experience His astounding love.

God's Agape Love Can Grow in Us— To Pass On to Others

Jesus taught that the second highest commandment is: *"You shall [agape] love your neighbor [those around you] as [you agape love] yourself"* (Mark 12:31). We need God's Spirit to give us His unique *agape* love in order to love others in God's way. We cannot produce this unique love on our own, nor can we pour it out to others just by our own efforts. We need the Spirit of Jesus within us, and also flowing out through us to others.

And just before His betrayal and crucifixion, Jesus said to His disciples, *"A new commandment I give to you, that you [agape] love one another; as I have [agape] loved you, that you also [agape] love one another"* (John 13:34). The commandment to love others *as* Jesus loved us is much greater than the commandment to love others *as* we love ourselves. He loved us more than He loved Himself. Pass this kind of Jesus–love on to fellow disciples of Jesus and to the world.

Pause for a moment to think of how greatly Jesus loved us when we were not worthy. His *agape* love is humanly impossible, but it is not impossible to the Spirit of God within us. His Holy Spirit grows this fruit of *agape* love in us—to share it with others.

> …the [*agape*] love of God has been poured out in our hearts by the Holy Spirit who was given to us. (Romans 5:5)

> But the fruit of the Spirit is [*agape*] love, joy, peace… (Galatians 5:22)

> And this commandment we have [received] from Him: that he who [*agape*] loves God must [*agape*] love his brother also. (1 John 4:21)

> …it is God who works in you both to will and to do for His good pleasure. (Philippians 2:13)

Agape Love is the Real Essence of God's Perfect Nature

Agape love is God's inner nature, His character, and His disposition. God is love right down to the depths of His Heart, and to the very core of His Being. He is total, perfect true love. He cannot be otherwise. This is the real Heart of God.

This is what God's everlasting Word says again and again. It is true. He cannot fail. He is faithful. He cannot lie. These are the promises of His love to us. We can trust them and act on them, totally. His *agape* love is far, far higher and greater than any other kind of love. This is the "Astounding Love"—far, far beyond measure!

LET'S ASK HIM:

> God, I'm so glad that the very essence of Your Heart is love—even for me! Please give me faith to believe it. I want to receive Your great love, and to receive You and Your Son, Jesus.
>
> Help me to turn my heart over to You completely. I want to be Your love–child forever. I want to deeply experience Your Father–love.
>
> Please, God, plant Your Spirit and Your love deep within me. Then live out Your love through me—to others.
>
> I take You at Your Word. I now receive Your promises. I receive You. I receive Your Son, Jesus. I receive Your Spirit. I receive Your great love.
>
> And I thank You God, very, very much. I want to love You in return—joyfully, with all my heart.
>
> I ask this in all the authority, power, and supremacy of Jesus' name.

CHAPTER NINE

EXPRESS DELIVERY: FROM GOD'S HEART TO OURS

God's Perfect Love for Us, in Action

LOVE MUST BE EXPRESSED—BY BOTH WORDS AND ACTIONS

An essential characteristic about love is that it has a very strong desire to express itself to the one it loves. Love without expression in words and actions is of no benefit. It is empty.

God is not just sitting up in heaven having nice, loving thoughts and feelings about us, while doing nothing about it. He has already supremely demonstrated His love to us on the cross. He expresses His love to us clearly in His Word. And He communicates it to us by action—lots of action. He expresses His love toward us in tangible ways right here on earth. He eagerly sends the outworking of His love to us, personally, via His own "express delivery" system. He has thousands of ways of doing so. Here in this chapter, from God's own Scriptures, are the main expressions of His great *agape* love—from His Heart to ours.

THE MAIN EXPRESSIONS OF GOD'S GREAT *AGAPE* LOVE

Perfect Mercy

On Mount Sinai, when God first revealed His inner nature, His real Heart, in His Scriptures, the first characteristic He spoke to Moses was, "I am merciful (full of mercy)" (Exodus 34:6). (See Chapter 2.)

The Hebrew word here for "mercy" is very rich and deep in meaning, and it is always used to refer to God's mercy, and to His only. This is the special and unique mercy of God. The connotation is abundant, extraordinary, and uncommon. It comes from a prime root that means to show tender love and affection, to show great compassion, great mercy, and great pity. It is also translated as "loving kindness" and "tender mercies." An extension of this prime root also means to cherish (treasure), as a woman cherishes the baby in her womb. This is deep inner affection. This is Who God is, deep within His Heart. This is the core and nature of His personality.

This is what God is saying here to you and me: "I am *full* (not partly full) of mercy. I am full of tender love, deep affection, great compassion, and great pity. Even before I created the world (Ephesians 1:4), I have cherished you in My womb (My Heart)." This is a very deep insight into the nature and character of God, and His disposition towards you and me, and *every* human on earth.

Basically, mercy is not getting what we, as sinners, rightfully deserve. It is giving undeserved favor to the guilty—free of charge. And we all need lots of God's mercy.

> ...for all have sinned and fall short of the glory of God. (Romans 3:23)

> As it is written: "There is none righteous, no, not one." (Romans 3:10)

God, because of His abundant, extraordinary love, compassion and pity, does not want us to get the condemnation and judgment we really do deserve. Look at what He says in His Word:

> For the wages of sin is [eternal] death, but the gift of God is eternal life in Christ Jesus our Lord. (Romans 6:23)

> The Lord is... not willing that any should perish but that all should come to repentance. (2 Peter 3:9)

> [God] desires all men [people] to be saved and to come to the knowledge of the truth. For there is one God and one Mediator between God and men [people], the Man Christ Jesus, who gave Himself a ransom for all... (1 Timothy 2:4–6)

This is the great and perfect love of God being expressed to us in tender mercy, loving kindness, and deep compassion and pity. He has great sympathy and empathy towards us. He is very sensitive to our feelings. He feels the hurt, the pain, and the emptiness within every one of us. He is not harsh, distant, unfeeling, and hard.

I will let God's Scriptures speak for themselves. These are

just a few of many verses that tell us God's mercy is great, rich, abundant, universal, and everlasting.

> He has not dealt with us according to our sins, nor punished us according to our iniquities. For as the heavens are high above the earth, so great is His mercy toward those who fear [revere] Him. (Psalm 103:10–11)

> …God… is rich in mercy, because of His great love with which He loved us. (Ephesians 2:4)

> …God… according to His abundant mercy has begotten [birthed] us again to a living hope through the resurrection of Jesus Christ from the dead. (1 Peter 1:3)

> The LORD is good to all, and His tender mercies are over all His works. (Psalm 145:9)

> But the mercy of the LORD is from everlasting to everlasting on those who fear [revere] Him. (Psalm 103:17)

Perfect Grace

The second thing God said to Moses on Mount Sinai was, "I am gracious (full of grace)" (Exodus 34:6). God's grace and mercy are like twin sisters. They are very closely related but are a little different. They make for a wonderful twofold expression of God's great love.

The Hebrew word here for "gracious" comes from a prime root meaning to bend, or stoop down, in kindness to someone inferior, in order to bestow favor. It is the very core nature and real Heart of Almighty God to humbly stoop down to us and bestow great favor upon us, even though we are extremely unworthy. Note that He is *full* of grace—not partly full, but entirely full.

Whereas mercy is *not* getting the judgment we really *do* deserve, grace is *getting* the favor that we really *do not* deserve. The definition of the Greek word for "grace" is free, undeserved favor, always a free gift. Grace cannot be earned, paid for, or paid back; if it could be, it would not be a free gift. It is not a loan or a mortgage; it is a gift.

Now, here is an illustration of how God's mercy and grace work together. Suppose you owe a million dollars to a friend who you treated very badly and deeply offended, but you lost your job and your health and became totally helpless. Therefore you became absolutely unable to pay this debt back to him. But this person is loving and compassionate, and full of tender mercy, forgiveness, kindness, and pity. So he, at great expense to himself, completely cancels the debt and lets you go totally free of it. This would be an act of great mercy. You are not getting what you really do deserve.

But although you would now be debt–free, you would be financially broke, utterly poverty–stricken, homeless, and about to starve to death.

Suppose that this wonderful loving friend is also full of grace. He loves you so much, regardless of the evil you did to him, that he opens a bank account in your name and deposits a million dollars in it for you. Then he comes to you and tells you that he has done this and that it is not a loan or a debt. He tells you that it is a completely free gift for you, and asks you if you will accept it—from his heart to yours. This would be an act of great grace. You are now being offered what you really do not deserve.

What would your answer be to him? Remember that you are helpless, poverty-stricken, and about to starve to death. Would you receive this great grace, or would you be too proud to accept this wonderful free love-gift?

This is exactly like God's mercy and grace. They are completely available to us, *if* we will humble ourselves, turn our heart back to Him, and receive, by simple child-like faith, His wonderful gift: Jesus—crucified for our forgiveness and resurrected for our justification (acquittal from guilt). What is your answer to God regarding His amazing offer to you?

God will not force His mercy and grace on anyone. This has to be willingly accepted and embraced, by faith. God must hear you answer "Yes," from a sincere and humble heart. It is your choice. God is greatly yearning to hear your "Yes!"

Hear what God says about His grace. Let His Word and His Spirit turn on the light deep inside your heart. God says His grace is exceedingly rich, abundant, and sufficient.

> ...He might show the exceeding riches of His grace in His kindness toward us in Christ Jesus. For by grace you have been saved through faith, and that not of yourselves; it is the gift of God, not of works, lest anyone should boast. (Ephesians 2:7–9)

> In Him [Jesus] we have redemption through His blood, the forgiveness of sins, according to the riches of His grace which He made to

abound toward us… (Ephesians 1:7–8)

But where sin abounded, grace abounded much more. (Romans 5:20)

My grace is sufficient for you, for My strength is made perfect in [your] weakness. (2 Corinthians 12:9)

Remember, this mercy and grace is not only what God has for us; this is also Who He is. This is what He is at the very center of His Heart. All His mercy and grace is an "express delivery" to us, of His great perfect love, because God is love— true love, beyond measure!

Perfect Patience

The third revelation God gave to Moses on Mount Sinai was, "I am longsuffering (full of patience)" (Exodus 34:6). This is the exact opposite of being short-tempered, quick-tempered, impatient, irritable, cranky, or easily and quickly provoked. "Longsuffering" means being lenient, patient, tolerant; and bearing and enduring offense for a long period of time.

For many years, satan told me that God was quite irritable and that sometimes He lost His temper. This deceiving enemy of ours would point out two incidences in Scripture where it appeared that God lost His temper and struck people down very quickly. Then satan would whisper into my heart, "See! That's what kind of a God He is. You'd better be really scared, 'cause you never know when He is suddenly going to lose His temper, and you will be 'ash in a flash.'" I tell you with all my heart, God is not like that, even if it appears sometimes that He is.

The first incidence that satan used was Uzzah, in 2 Samuel 6:1–8. Uzzah reached out his hand to steady the holy ark of God, to keep it from falling off an oxcart, and immediately God struck him dead. The second incidence was Ananias and his wife, Sapphira, in Acts 5:1–10. All they did was lie to the Holy Spirit in order to appear to people to be more spiritual and dedicated than they really were. And they died immediately—right there on the spot.

Yes, it looks like God was very quick-tempered on those two occasions, and that He lost His cool, but we must never form our opinion of God from just two isolated incidences, because we do not know all the details and the preceding circumstances of these people and how long God had already been dealing with them in patience. Even if God decided to act quickly in order to make them an example to others, that is His sovereign right, and He will judge them graciously and righteously. But Scripture is very clear that God does not act impatiently. He cannot. It is not His nature.

We must not form our belief in God from these two historical incidences—especially when satan's interpretation of them contradicts the clear and plain statements of divine Scripture. Look at what God Himself says in His Word about His longsuffering and patience:

> But You, O Lord, are a God full of compassion, and gracious, longsuffering and abundant in mercy and truth. (Psalm 86:15)

> The LORD is merciful and gracious, slow to anger, and abounding in mercy. (Psalm 103:8)

The Lord is not slack concerning His promise, as some count slackness, but is longsuffering toward us, not willing that any should perish but that all should come to repentance. (2 Peter 3:9)

Or do you despise the riches of His goodness, forbearance, and longsuffering, not knowing that the goodness of God leads you to repentance? (Romans 2:4)

[*Agape*] Love suffers long and is kind... is not [easily] provoked... (1 Corinthians 13:4–5)

But the fruit of the Spirit is love, joy, peace, longsuffering, kindness, goodness... (Galatians 5:22)

But You are God, ready to pardon, gracious and merciful, slow to anger, abundant in kindness... (Nehemiah 9:17)

God's perfect longsuffering and patience means that His perfect mercy and grace toward us go on and on and on for a very long time. How wonderful! This is a further express delivery to us of God's perfect love, the very core of His nature, His true Heart.

Perfect Goodness

The next part that God revealed about His real Heart is, "I am abounding in goodness" (Exodus 34:6). The Hebrew word here for "goodness" is very close in meaning to mercy and grace. It means kindness, gentleness, tenderness, to show favor, to benefit, and be advantageous. It is also translated as "loving kindness" and "merciful kindness." The word "goodness" in English means to be favorable to, beneficial to, and advantageous to another person.

So contrary to what satan has said to so many of us, God is not harsh, hard, cold, distant, and unfeeling. He is kind, gentle, tender, warm, and wanting to do good to us.

But notice that God said that He is *abounding* in goodness. Now, "abounding" means exceedingly full, plenteous, and to multiply by the myriad. He is not only full of mercy and full of grace, but He is full to overflowing with goodness—like a river of kindness, tenderness, favor, and benefit overflowing its banks and flowing toward us, for our advantage. This flows from the very center of His being, His real Heart, because God *is* love—beyond measure.

Listen to what God says about His goodness, and ask God to help you believe what He says in His Word:

> The LORD is good to all, and His tender mercies are over all His works. (Psalm 145:9)

> Oh, how great is Your goodness, which You have laid up for those who fear [revere] You. (Psalm 31:19)

> The goodness of God endures continually. (Psalm 52:1)

> Or do you despise the riches of His goodness, forbearance, and longsuffering, not knowing that the goodness of God leads you to repentance? (Romans 2:4)

God has many, many ways of expressing His goodness to us, including *provision* and *blessing*. These are two important promises that He has made, again and again, in His Word.

Provision

God has promised to provide for us, His children. He is very big-hearted and generous. He is not miserly or stingy. Look at what He says to us:

> Blessed be the Lord, who daily loads us with benefits. (Psalm 68:19)

> And my God shall supply all your need according to His riches in glory by Christ Jesus. (Philippians 4:19)

> And God is able to make all grace abound toward you, that you, always having all sufficiency in all things, may have an abundance for every good work. (2 Corinthians 9:8)

> Now if God so clothes the grass of the field, which today is, and tomorrow is thrown into the oven, will He not much more clothe you, O you of little faith? (Matthew 6:30)

Blessing

This word "blessing" is used often in Scripture, so I decided to look up its original meaning in the Hebrew language. I found that it means to bend the knee, to kneel. Now, I was really puzzled by this. What has bending the knee got to do with blessing? So I studied further and found that this word was used when someone would give a gift to a very important person, such as a tribal chief or a king. As they would give the gift, they would kneel to also give great honor and respect to that person. This is close to the Hebrew meaning of "grace."

I can understand using this word in the context of us blessing God, but the Bible, many times, uses this word when God blesses us. How can this be? How can God bend down to us and give us such honor and respect? I wrestled with this for a few minutes. Suddenly it dawned on me—a flash of revelation from the Spirit of God. I had a thought that had never occurred to me before: *the humility of God.*

The Humility of God

This is absolutely astounding! Satan had put a thought into my mind many times before—namely, "God must be some kind of big, proud, super-ego sitting on His throne in Heaven and telling us all to bow down, praise Him, worship Him, and keep on telling Him how good and wonderful He is." This thought bothered me every time, but I didn't know what to say against it.

But suddenly I had the answer to satan's slanderous lie. I saw the humility of God. It is absolutely astounding! Look at it for yourself:

> And without controversy great is the mystery of godliness: God was manifested in the flesh...
> (1 Timothy 3:16)

> [Jesus], being in the form of God, did not consider it robbery to be equal with God, but made

Himself of no reputation, taking the form of a bondservant [slave], and coming in the likeness of men. And being found in appearance as a man, He humbled Himself and became obedient to the point of death, even the death of the cross. (Philippians 2:6–8)

For Christ also suffered once for sins, the just for the unjust, that He might bring us to God, being put to death in the flesh but made alive by the Spirit. (1 Peter 3:18)

…God, having raised up His Servant Jesus, sent Him to bless you in turning away every one of you from your iniquities. (Acts 3:26)

God did bend the knee. He bowed down, and *down*, and **down** to the depths of where we were in our sin, and became the atonement for all our sins. He loved us all so much that He humbled Himself to that unimaginable extent so that He could forgive us, cleanse us, embrace us, and have us in close, loving fellowship with Him forever.

God bends the knee every day in many, many ways to bless us again and again. He is the source of and the perfect and ultimate example of all true humility. Jesus' humility is supernatural. By His Spirit now dwelling within us, He can give us His supernatural humility.

Go back, for a moment, to the previous chapter, and look again at the thirty statements under the heading "The High Price God Paid to Win Us Back to Himself," and see His great humility, how far down He stooped—from the highest glories of Heaven to the lowest depths of hell.

God not only gave us His precious gift of forgiveness and salvation, but by bending the knee down to us, He also bestowed on us great honor and incredible value. Just meditate on "The High Price God Paid to Win Us Back to Himself." We are unimaginably precious to Him!

Don't ever let satan or anyone else make you feel worthless, like just a piece of human junk. This accusation is a horrible lie. You and I are a highly esteemed treasure to God. We are a delight to His real Heart. He cherishes us greatly. We are incredibly valuable to Him. To God, every one of us is worth all the shame and pain Jesus suffered, and every drop of blood He shed for us on that cross.

When we do turn and come back to Him and receive Him, He calls us His spiritual children, and He makes us coworkers with Him and ambassadors of His kingdom. What a high honor He bestows upon us! What an incredible significance He gives to us! Listen to what God says:

> Behold what manner of [*agape*] love the Father has bestowed on us, that we should be called children of God! (1 John 3:1)

> You have made him [mankind] a little lower than the angels; You have crowned him with glory and honor, and set him over the works of Your hands. (Hebrews 2:7)

> The Spirit Himself bears witness with our spirit that we are children of God, and if children, then heirs—heirs of God and joint heirs with Christ,

if indeed we suffer with Him, that we may also be glorified together. (Romans 8:16–17)

For we are God's fellow workers; you are God's field, you are God's building… Do you not know that you are the temple of God and that the Spirit of God dwells in you? (1 Corinthians 3:9, 16)

To Him [Jesus] who loved us and washed us from our sins in His own blood, and has made us kings and priests to His God and Father, to Him be glory and dominion forever and ever. (Revelation 1:5–6)

Now then, we are ambassadors for Christ… (2 Corinthians 5:20)

All of His perfect provision, blessing, and humility are express deliveries to us of God's great goodness, flowing freely from His loving Heart. This is what He is deep within His nature and character.

Perfect Forgiveness

The fifth thing God revealed to Moses on Mount Sinai about His real Heart of love was *"forgiving iniquity and transgression and sin"* (Exodus 34:7).

God uses three different Hebrew words to cover the scope of His forgiveness:

- The first word God uses here is *avon*, translated "iniquity," which means perversity, and deviation from what is right.

- The second word is *pesha*, translated "transgression," which means rebellion, breaking the bounds, and trespassing.

- The third word is *chattaah*, translated "sin," which means to miss the mark, to break the law, and to offend.

God deliberately uses these three different words, which cover the whole range of human moral and spiritual failure, to let us know that He is eager and willing to forgive all the wrong which we do. He is not reluctant to freely and completely pardon us. He does not grudgingly forgive. He is eager!

"Forgiveness" is translated from a Hebrew word meaning to lift up (or off), to bear anyone's sin (to receive the punishment of another's sin upon one's self), to take away anyone's sin (to make atonement for sin). This is exactly what Jesus did for us when He died on that cross and carried our sins upon His own soul, all the way to the depths of hell.

Because Jesus has completely paid (atoned) for all our sins, God can legally, justly, and righteously lift from each of us all our guilt and condemnation and freely forgive us completely.

"Forgive" in English means to fully pardon, to cease demanding punishment, to drop all accusations and all charges. This is the whole point of God coming to us as man, born of a virgin, then dying for the sins of His entire human race. He wants us to be reconciled unto Himself through the shed blood of Jesus Christ. God can righteously and justly forgive each of us totally because the full price has already been paid by Jesus.

God has written much in His Word about His forgiveness. Read it, and believe it:

> For You, Lord, are good, and ready [willing and eager] to forgive, and abundant in mercy to all those who call upon You. (Psalm 86:5)

> ...But You are God, ready to pardon, gracious and merciful, slow to anger, abundant in kindness, and did not forsake them. (Nehemiah 9:17)

> I will cleanse them from all their iniquity by which they have sinned against Me, and I will pardon all their iniquities by which they have sinned and by which they have transgressed against Me. (Jeremiah 33:8)

> Let the wicked forsake his way, and the unrighteous man [person] his thoughts; let him return to the Lord, and He will have mercy on him; and to our God, for He will abundantly pardon. (Isaiah 55:7)

> I, even I, am He who blots out your transgressions for My own sake; and I will not remember your sins. (Isaiah 43:25)

> I have blotted out, like a thick cloud, your transgressions, and like a cloud, your sins. Return to Me, for I have redeemed you. (Isaiah 44:22)

As far as the east is from the west, so far has He removed our transgressions from us. (Psalm 103:12)

Who is a God like You, pardoning iniquity and passing over the transgression of the remnant of His heritage [His people]? He does not retain His anger forever, because He delights in mercy. He will again have compassion on us, and will subdue our iniquities. You will cast all our sins into the depths of the sea. (Micah 7:18–19)

Wash me, and I shall be whiter than snow. (Psalm 51:7)

If we confess our sins [express repentance], He is faithful and just to forgive us our sins and to cleanse us from all unrighteousness. (1 John 1:9)

...through this Man [Jesus] is preached to you the forgiveness of sins; and by Him everyone who believes is justified from all things... (Acts 13:38–39)

In Him [Jesus] we have redemption through His blood, the forgiveness of sins, according to the riches of His grace. (Ephesians 1:7)

Notice that God has promised to blot out our sins. They are deleted from the records of the Supreme Court of the Universe. God has promised not to bring them to remembrance ever again. When we receive, by faith, the redemption of Jesus Christ and His forgiveness, our criminal record is blotted out forever.

This is what the Scriptures call "justification," which means legal and formal acquittal from guilt. God, as Judge, pronounces the repentant sinner as righteous.

> ...being justified freely by His grace through the redemption that is in Christ Jesus, whom God set forth as a propitiation [payment] by His blood, through faith, to demonstrate His righteousness... that He might be just and the justifier of the one who has faith in Jesus. (Romans 3:24–26)

> Therefore, having been justified by faith, we have peace with God through our Lord Jesus Christ. (Romans 5:1)

> Much more then, having been justified by His blood, we shall be saved from wrath through Him. (Romans 5:9)

Christ's perfect redemption, and God's perfect forgiveness and complete justification, are wondrous expressions of the aims and objectives of His true, great Heart of love for us. This is Who He is and Who He always will be. God cannot be, nor can He act, differently than the very core of His actual nature, character, and Heart. He is forever faithful.

The Parable of the Passionate Papa

This is my favorite parable of all the parables Jesus used, because it illustrates the passionate, compassionate, loving, forgiving Heart of God our Father so wonderfully. It has been called the Parable of the Prodigal Son, but I call it the Parable of the Passionate Papa, because it is more about the passionate love of the father for his son than about the lostness of his son. This parable shows God's perfect mercy, grace, patience, goodness, and forgiveness all combined together in a wonderful way.

In Luke 15:1–2, the sinners and outcasts came to Jesus to hear Him, but the proud, super–religious people grumbled and criticized Him, saying, *"This Man receives sinners and eats with them."* So Jesus gave them three similar parables: the lost sheep, the lost coin, and the lost son. But it is the one about the lost son that gives us a much deeper insight into the great loving Father–Heart of God:

> A certain man had two sons.
>
> And the younger of them said to his father, "Father, give me the portion of goods [inheritance] that falls to me." So he divided to them his livelihood.
>
> And not many days after, the younger son gathered all together, journeyed to a far country, and there wasted his possessions with prodigal [extravagant, lavish] living.
>
> But when he had spent all, there arose a severe famine in that land, and he began to be in want [need]… and no one gave him anything.

> But when he came to himself [his senses],
> he said, "How many of my father's hired ser-
> vants have bread [food] enough and to spare,
> and I perish with hunger! I will arise and go to
> my father, and will say to him, 'Father, I have
> sinned against heaven and before you, and I am
> no longer worthy to be called your son. Make
> me like one of your hired servants.'"
>
> And he arose and came to his father. (Luke
> 15:11–14, 16–20).

Before God showed me His wonderful loving Heart, I would have imagined that the father would stand to his full height at the top of the front steps, with his arms folded across his chest and a frown on his face, and wait until the son came near. Then he would say, "Stop right there. How dare you come back here after disgracing the family name and squandering your inheritance! What a ragged, barefoot, filthy, stinking mess you are. Why are you here?"

But the father did not respond like that. Look at what the father actually did, and you will see the great passion and burning unconditional love of God's Heart for us—expressed in incredible mercy, grace, patience, goodness, and forgiveness:

> But when he was still a great way off, his father
> saw him and had compassion, and ran and fell
> on his neck [embraced him] and kissed him.
>
> And the son said to him, "Father, I have
> sinned against heaven and in your sight, and
> am no longer worthy to be called your son."

> But the father [interrupting the son's prepared speech] said to his servants, "Bring out the best robe and put it on him, and put a ring on his hand and sandals on his feet. And bring the fatted calf here and kill it, and let us eat and be merry; for this my son was dead and is alive again; he was lost and is found." And they began to be merry. (Luke 15:20–24)

From this Scripture, I believe that the father was constantly looking down the road to the horizon day after day, longing, yearning, grieving, crying, hoping, and praying. And one day, when he recognized that the distant, ragged, staggering figure on the horizon was his son, he leapt off the front porch and raced down the road to welcome him home. I can imagine the servants were running after him but couldn't catch up to him. Likely, Mama was afraid he would have a heart attack.

I'm sure the son was filthy and smelly, but the father reached out to him, hugged him, and kissed him on both cheeks, regardless of the dirt, rags, sweat, and stench. Upon his son's confession, he instantly forgave him, restored him, and ordered a big party to celebrate. He invited all his friends, neighbors, and relatives. And if you know anything about Hebrew dancing, they were celebrating vigorously. This illustrates the true Heart of our loving Heavenly Father—passionately welcoming us, His straying children, back home and into His great big loving arms.

This straying son did not realize the greatness of his father's heart of compassionate and his white–hot burning love. He was just desperately hoping to get a lowly job and maybe sleep in the barn. He never imagined that he would receive such an exuberant, lavish, loving, and joyous welcome, and such an enthusiastic forgiveness and restoration.

But the elder son (the super–religious one) was angry and highly offended and would not go inside to join the party. He complained that his father was honoring the younger son who had *"devoured [the father's] livelihood with harlots"* (Luke 15:30). So His father came out and pleaded with him. Obviously, this son *also* did not know the great loving heart of his father, even though he had stayed home and had worked faithfully. There are many "faithful" Christians who still do *not* realize the astounding greatness of their Father's love.

Jesus gave the meaning of these three parables: *"…there is joy in the presence of the angels of God over one sinner who repents"* (Luke 15:10). Don't ever be afraid to come back to God, no matter how badly you may have sinned. When you sincerely repent from your heart, He will rush out to embrace you, cleanse you, restore you, and celebrate!

Perfect Jealousy

Yes, jealousy is an expression of the astounding, loving Heart of God. This may startle you. It startled me at first. Then God began to open the eyes of my heart to see that this characteristic of jealousy embraces both "God is love" (Chapters 8 and 9) and "God is light" (the next two chapters).

When God opened up His inner nature and revealed His great goodness to Moses on Mount Sinai (see Chapter 2 and Exodus 34:5–7), He added this: *"…you shall worship no other god, for the Lord, whose name is Jealous, is a jealous God"*

(Exodus 34:14).

God is so serious about this command against idolatry that He has even given Himself the name "Jealous" as one of His many titles. A little over forty days previously, God had spoken the Ten Commandments to Israel in that awesome, booming, ground–shaking voice from Mount Sinai, and He had made this very thing the first and second commandments, because of His jealousy:

> You shall have no other gods before [besides] Me. You shall not make for yourself a carved image—any likeness of anything... you shall not bow down to them nor serve them. For I, the LORD your God, am a jealous God... (Exodus 20:3–5)

> Thus says the LORD of hosts: "I am zealous [jealous] for Zion [God's people] with great zeal; with great fervor I am zealous for her." (Zechariah 8:2)

> They [God's people] provoked Him to jealousy with foreign gods. (Deuteronomy 32:16)

Many other times in Scripture, God says He is jealous and He has jealousy because of our idolatries.

Giving our highest love, worship, or priority to any other person or thing is, in God's eyes, idolatry. Scripture makes it very plain that idolatry is spiritual adultery against God Himself. As we will see, it is also breaking the New Covenant, which He made with us in Christ. And that is very, very serious!

Now, when we fallen, sinful humans think of jealousy, we

usually think of an ugly, bitter, and sometimes violent, vengeful emotion. How can God be jealous and still be love? Can God actually have perfect, loving jealousy?

Yes! Absolutely yes! God is not contaminated with sin like we are. He is eternally, infinitely, and totally perfect love. Therefore His jealousy is not destructive and evil. It is not murderous, as human jealousy sometimes gets. Our idolatries deeply grieve and anger His Heart, but His jealousy is always good, righteous, loving, and just.

Let me illustrate how jealousy is an expression of God's love. My wife and I were married for fifty–three years before she went home to heaven. We loved each other very much. When we married, we vowed (covenanted) before God, our family, and friends that we would keep ourselves only for each other as long as we both lived. If either of us had given our affection, or ourselves, to someone else, our spouse would have been deeply hurt and rightly jealous, because the covenant–love that should have only been going to them was being *misplaced* on someone else.

Why would we have felt that way? Because we loved each other so much! If we had not loved each other, we would not have cared, nor been jealous. We would have just shrugged our shoulders and said, "It doesn't matter to me." But because we loved each other so much, and because our spouse's love was so very precious to us, we would have been deeply hurt. We would rightly have been offended, because that love and affection was being poured out *illegitimately* on someone else. Our heart would have been crying out, "It is wrong! It is unjust! You are breaking your vows, your covenant, to me! I love you! I want you back! I want you back!"

In the Old Testament (Covenant), God related to the nation of Israel as their Father, but He also likened Himself to being their Husband. As such, He loved them (and still does) in a very special way, and their love for Him was very, very precious to Him. Giving their worship, their love, or their allegiance to any other god, thing, or person amounted to spiritual *adultery*. It grieved Him deeply—because He loved them so very much.

God's immeasurable love for us is so great that He does *not* desire just a casual friendship with us. His burning, passionate love longs for a covenant–love relationship, an eternal marriage–covenant relationship with us. He has provided, through the shed blood of His Son Jesus, that kind of relationship, and called it the New Covenant.

In the New Testament (Covenant), God revealed Himself through Jesus, and made Jesus to be our Heavenly Bridegroom. As believers, we are engaged (covenanted) to be spiritually married to Christ. The Spirit of God was speaking through the apostle Paul when Paul wrote to those whom he had led to faith in Christ:

> For I am jealous for you with godly jealousy.
> For I have betrothed you [made a binding covenant] to one husband, that I may present you
> as a chaste virgin to Christ. (2 Corinthians 11:2)

Marriage is a very high and strong covenant. A covenant is much stronger and more binding than just a promise. Our receiving Jesus is a spiritual union with Him, and our spiritual union with Jesus is a marriage–covenant—"The New Covenant." His Spirit is married (entwined) with our spirits by the New Covenant, which He has made with us through His shed blood.

God's love is incredibly strong and intense. It is very great and pure. God is also absolutely true, righteous, and just. He *cannot* lie. He will *never* break His new love–covenant with us! God really means business about us giving back to Him our full, total, undiluted, undivided, and faithful love, but He knows that we fallen humans *cannot*, by our own power, keep such a love–covenant with Him. So, as part of the New Covenant, through the crucifixion and shed blood of His Son, Jesus, God made a way for us to keep covenant with Him.

In the New Covenant, God not only cleanses us from all our filthiness and idols but also gives us a new heart, puts His Spirit within us, and puts His law in our minds and in our hearts. Look at what God prophesied in the Old Testament, and is now fulfilling for us in Christ, in the New Covenant:

> Behold, the days are coming, says the LORD, when I will make a new covenant with the house of Israel… not according to the covenant that I made with their fathers in the day that I took them by the hand to lead them out of the land of Egypt, My covenant which they broke, though I was a husband to them, says the LORD. But this is the covenant that I will make with the house of Israel… I will put My law in their minds, and write it on their hearts; and I will be their God, and they shall be My people. (Jeremiah 31:31–33)

Then I will sprinkle clean water on you, and you shall be clean; I will cleanse you from all your filthiness and from all your idols. I will give you a new heart and put a new spirit within you;... I will put My Spirit within you and cause you to walk in My statutes, and you will keep My judgments and do them. (Ezekiel 36:25–27)

Therefore, if anyone is in Christ, he is a new creation; old things have [are] passed away; behold, all things have [are] become new. (2 Corinthians 5:17)

And as they were eating, Jesus took bread, blessed and broke it, and gave it to the disciples and said, "Take, eat; this is My body." Then He took the cup, and gave thanks, and gave it to them, saying, "Drink from it, all of you. For this is My blood of the new covenant, which is shed for many for the remission [forgiveness] of sins." (Matthew 26:26–28)

It is Jesus' Spirit, united (married) with our spirit, which enables (empowers) us to keep His commands (covenant) and do them. He, within us, keeps the New Covenant for us by *His* victory and *His* power—not ours.

This is extremely good news for all of us failing humans! God freely offers all of Jesus' resurrection life to us as a wedding gift for our covenant–marriage to His Beloved Son, Jesus! God's great, astounding love is the only explanation for Him making such a covenant with us!

Our love is more precious to Him than we can ever comprehend. If we give our worship, our highest love, our top priority to anything or anyone else, we are committing spiritual adultery against the Most High God and against His Son, Jesus Christ. His Heart will cry out to us, again and again,

"You are breaking your covenant with Me! I love you! I want you back! I pour out My total love upon you, and I long for you to pour back your total love exclusively upon Me. I don't want just your belief and faith in Me. I don't want just your work and service. I don't want just your acts of sacrifice. I want nothing less than your total, faithful love, poured out on Me, and on Me alone (see Mark 12:28–30). And I won't be satisfied with anything less. I'll pursue you to the very gates of hell, if I have to, in order to win your love back to Me, because I love you so very much and I don't want to lose you. I, and only I, am the Supreme God. All other gods and priorities are idols, and are detrimental and destructive to you. I don't want your destruction. I want only the best for you. I'll cry out to you, 'I want you back! I want you to keep the covenant that we vowed to each other!'"

This expression of jealousy is a passionate expression of God's love for us. Remember, though, that God is not just "love" (1 John 4:8, 16); He is also "light" (1 John 1:5). "Light" is a metaphor in Scripture for truth, faithfulness, righteousness, and justice. God hates unfaithfulness, unrighteousness, and injustice!

Unfaithfulness to God (idolatry) is putting something else in God's place. Anything can become an idol if we love it more than we love God: money, power, prestige, success, comfort, pleasure, possessions, church, spouse, family, friends, and especially *our own selves*.

Idolatry not only violates God's great Heart of love for us, but it also violates His great Heart of truth, faithfulness, righteousness, and justice. Idolatry violates His New Covenant with us, who are His bride. It is unrighteous and unjust.

God alone is our Creator, our Father, our King, our Lord, our Lover, our Husband, and our Redeemer. We belong to Him, to Him only, and to no one else. We don't even belong to ourselves (see 1 Corinthians 6:19–20). Only He is the rightful recipient of *all* our highest love, worship, devotion, submission, and service.

> ...that He [Jesus] alone in everything and in every respect might occupy the chief place (stand first and be preeminent). (Colossians 1:18, AMP)

Anything less is wrong. Anything else is rebellious and unjust. Anything else is breaking covenant with Him. Anything else is a sin of the greatest magnitude. God calls it iniquity!

Idolatry of any kind provokes God to jealousy—a loving jealousy and a righteous jealousy. His jealousy will cry out to us, "Your idolatry is wrong. It is iniquity. It will deceive you. It will destroy you. I love you! I love you! I want you back! I want your love back! I am your covenant–husband!"

Yes, jealousy is an intense and passionate expression of God's burning Heart of love. It is also an intense, passionate, burning expression of "God is light," which introduces us to the next two chapters.

Let's Ask Him:

> God, thank You. Thank You. Thank You for expressing Your great love to me in such wonderful ways.
>
> Help me believe completely all of Your mercy, grace, longsuffering, goodness, and forgiveness. Help me receive whole–heartedly the express deliveries of Your love.
>
> As I grow spiritually, cause me to experience more and more of Your great love.
>
> Thank You, Jesus, for not just staying up in heaven, but for coming down to me and dying for my sins. Thank You for rising from the dead to justify me and to become my victorious, living Savior, my loving Friend, and my perfect, passionate Bridegroom.
>
> Help me to express my love and gratitude back to You more and more. Empower me to love you totally and to remain totally faithful to You, my Beloved Husband.
>
> I ask this in all the authority of Jesus' name, which is far above every other name.

CHAPTER TEN

THE LIGHT—FAR, FAR ABOVE ALL LIGHT

Perfect Light—Beyond Measure

God is not only perfect love (1 John 4:8, 16); He is also perfect "light" (1 John 1:5). Just as love is the very essence of God's nature, so also is light. They are always, totally combined.

Remember that when God revealed His goodness to Moses on Mount Sinai (see Chapter 2), it was an integrated combination of love and light. They are inseparable. Both are essential, and they perfectly balance each other. God's truth, righteousness, and justice in no way detract from or diminish His love, mercy, grace, and forgiveness. In fact, His light accentuates and guarantees the genuineness and faithfulness of His great, eternal *agape* love.

GOD IS PERFECT LIGHT

This is the message which we have heard from Him and declare to you, that God is light and in Him is no darkness at all. If we say that we have fellowship with Him, and walk in darkness, we lie and do not practice the truth. But if we walk in the light as He is in the light, we have fellowship with one another, and the blood of Jesus Christ His Son cleanses us from all sin. (1 John 1:5–7)

God uses the word "light" here as a metaphor for truth, faithfulness, righteousness, and justice. Notice that light is what God is, at the very center of His being, not just what He has or what He gives. God Himself is absolute truth, faithfulness, righteousness, and justice to the very core of His being.

THE MAIN CHARACTERISTICS OF "GOD IS LIGHT"

Perfect Truth

The definition of "truth" is complete, consistent adherence to the facts, to one's promises, and to reality; verity, fidelity, genuineness, and total integrity. God's perfect truth is absolute, abounding, great, unfailing, and everlasting. Jesus is the embodiment and the ultimate demonstration (expression) of God's truth. Here is what God Himself says about this in His own Word, the Bible:

> He is the Rock, His work is perfect; for all His ways are justice, a God of truth and without injustice; righteous and upright is He. (Deuteronomy 32:4)

> And the LORD passed before him and proclaimed, "The LORD, the LORD God, merciful and gracious, longsuffering, and abounding in goodness and truth." (Exodus 34:6)

> For Your mercy reaches unto the heavens, and Your truth unto the clouds. (Psalm 57:10)

Thus God, determining to show more abundantly to the heirs of promise the immutability of His counsel, confirmed it by an oath, that by two immutable [unchangeable] things, in which it is impossible for God to lie, we might have strong consolation, who have fled for refuge to lay hold of the hope set before us. (Hebrews 6:17–18)

For His merciful kindness is great toward us, and the truth of the LORD endures forever. Praise the LORD! (Psalm 117:2)

And the Word [Jesus] became flesh and dwelt among us, and we beheld His glory, the glory as of the only begotten of the Father, full of grace and truth. (John 1:14)

Jesus said to him, "I am the way, the truth, and the life. No one comes to the Father except through Me." (John 14:6)

So every part of God's nature and character is absolutely and eternally true. This means that His great, immeasurable, perfect love is eternally true. We can confidently believe in, trust in, and depend upon God's wonderful love for each of us personally.

Perfect Faithfulness

The definition of "faithful" or "faithfulness" is trustworthy, unfailing, unwavering, continuing in truth and in righteousness, unfailing truth, keeping one's word, one's promises, and one's covenant. God's faithfulness is absolute, great, unwavering, unfailing, and everlasting. Read what God has written in His Scriptures regarding His perfect faithfulness:

> Therefore know that the LORD your God, He is God, the faithful God who keeps covenant and mercy for a thousand generations with those who love Him and keep His commandments. (Deuteronomy 7:9)

> Through the LORD's mercies we are not consumed, because His compassions fail not. They are new every morning; great is Your faithfulness. (Lamentations 3:22–23)

> If we are faithless, He remains faithful; He cannot deny Himself. (2 Timothy 2:13)

> Nevertheless My lovingkindness I will not utterly take from him, nor allow My faithfulness to fail. My covenant I will not break, nor alter the word that has gone out of My lips. (Psalm 89:33–34)

> Forever, O LORD, Your word is settled in heaven. Your faithfulness endures to all generations; You established the earth, and it abides. (Psalm 119:89–90)

So, all of God's great goodness—His love and His light combined—will never fail. Indeed, they can never, ever fail.

God cannot violate His own nature. How utterly wonderful! He will always faithfully and truly love us—beyond measure!

Perfect Righteousness

The definition of "righteousness" is right–ness, upright, virtuous, blameless, and just. God's righteousness is absolute, great, passionate, total, and everlasting. Listen to what God is saying to us in His everlasting Word. These are just a few of many Scriptures about God's righteousness:

> The fear [reverence] of the LORD is clean, enduring forever; the judgments of the LORD are true and righteous altogether. (Psalm 19:9)

> Your mercy, O LORD, is in the heavens; Your faithfulness reaches to the clouds. Your righteousness is like the great mountains; Your judgments are a great deep; O LORD, You preserve man and beast. (Psalm 36:5–6)

> "But let him who glories glory in this, that he understands and knows Me, that I am the LORD, exercising lovingkindness, judgment, and righteousness in the earth. For in these I delight," says the LORD. (Jeremiah 9:24)

> The LORD is righteous in all His ways, gracious in all His works. (Psalm 145:17)

> Your righteousness is an everlasting righteousness, and Your law is truth. (Psalm 119:142)

So, all of God's great goodness will also be absolutely righteous and everlastingly pure—real true love. He will not, and cannot, ever do us any wrong.

Perfect Justice

The definition of "justice" is adherence to truth, impartiality, right–ness, fairness, equity, rendering what is right, rightly due, or merited (deserved). God's perfect justice is foundational, true, absolute, passionate, unfailing, and impartial. It is so important that we see and believe what God Himself says about His justice in His own Scriptures, and not what people say about it, nor what satan says to twist and misinterpret it.

> Righteousness and justice are the foundation of Your throne; mercy and truth go before Your face. (Psalm 89:14)

> But we know that the judgment of God is according to truth against those who practice such things [sins]. (Romans 2:2)

> He is the Rock, His work is perfect; for all His ways are justice, a God of truth and without injustice; righteous and upright is He. (Deuteronomy 32:4)

> "But let him who glories glory in this, that he understands and knows Me, that I am the LORD, exercising lovingkindness, judgment, and righteousness in the earth. For in these I delight," says the LORD. (Jeremiah 9:24)

The LORD is righteous in her midst, He will do
no unrighteousness. Every morning He brings
His justice to light; He never fails, but the unjust knows no shame. (Zephaniah 3:5)

For the LORD your God is God of gods and
Lord of lords, the great God, mighty and awesome, who shows no partiality nor takes a
bribe. He administers justice for the fatherless
and the widow, and loves the stranger [foreign-
er], giving him food and clothing. (Deuteronomy 10:17–18)

For there is no partiality with God. (Romans
2:11).

Then Peter opened his mouth and said: "In
truth I perceive that God shows no partiality.
But in every nation whoever fears [reveres]
Him and works righteousness is accepted by
Him." (Acts 10:34–35)

God shows personal favoritism to no man
[person]… (Galatians 2:6)

The Recompense of God

It is important to notice that recompense may be positive or
negative, resulting either in rewards or in loss, depending
upon what our deeds, words, and heart motives have been.

Do not be deceived, God is not mocked; for
whatever a man sows, that he will also reap. For

he who sows to his flesh will of the flesh reap corruption, but he who sows to the Spirit will of the Spirit reap everlasting life. (Galatians 6:7–8)

Also to You, O Lord, belongs mercy; for You render to each one according to his work. (Psalm 62:12)

I, the LORD, search the heart, I test the mind, even to give every man according to his ways, according to the fruit of his doings. (Jeremiah 17:10)

God will always be as merciful as He can possibly be. If we have sincerely repented and received His mercy and the forgiveness that Jesus paid for by His crucifixion and resurrection, then we will not receive what we rightly deserve for our sins, because Jesus has already paid the full price on His cross. God will be *delighted* to give us all the rewards He can for the faithfulness and good that He, by His grace and by His Spirit, has enabled us to do. He *"made him [mankind] a little lower than the angels... [and] crowned him [us] with glory and honor"* (Hebrews 2:7). This is what He originally had in mind for all His children. Therefore, He will be very happy to reward us for our faithfulness.

But if we have not turned back to God and have not received His mercy and forgiveness through Jesus' crucifixion, then He has to accept our decision on this. God will not violate our free will. We have given Him no other choice. He cannot violate His sense of justice. We will then have to receive the judgment we rightly deserve, even though Jesus has already paid for it with His shed blood. It is up to our decisions and our actions, not His. What a terrible tragedy for a person to be punished for his sin in spite of the fact that Jesus has already completely taken all of his punishment.

> But in accordance with your hardness and your impenitent heart you are treasuring up for yourself wrath in the day of wrath and revelation of the righteous judgment of God, who "will render to each one according to his deeds": eternal life to those who by patient continuance in doing good seek for glory, honor, and immortality; but to those who are self-seeking and do not obey the truth, but obey unrighteousness—indignation and wrath, tribulation and anguish, on every soul of man who does evil... (Romans 2:5–9)

> For the Son of Man will come in the glory of His Father with His angels, and then He will reward each according to his works. (Matthew 16:27)

> For we must all appear before the judgment seat of Christ, that each one may receive the things done in the body, according to what he has done, whether good or bad. (2 Corinthians 5:10)

> And as it is appointed for men to die once, but after this the judgment, so Christ was offered once to bear the sins of many. (Hebrews 9:27–28)

For there is nothing hidden which will not be revealed, nor has anything been kept secret but that it should come to light. (Mark 4:22)

Do not marvel at this; for the hour is coming in which all who are in the graves will hear His voice and come forth—those who have done good, to the resurrection of life, and those who have done evil, to the resurrection of condemnation. (John 5:28–29)

Then I saw a great white throne and Him who sat on it, from whose face the earth and the heaven fled away. And there was found no place for them. And I saw the dead, small and great, standing before God, and books were opened. And another book was opened, which is the Book of Life. And the dead were judged according to their works, by the things which were written in the books. The sea gave up the dead who were in it, and Death and Hades [hell] delivered up the dead who were in them. And they were judged, each one according to his works. Then Death and Hades [hell] were cast into the lake of fire. This is the second death. And anyone not found written in the Book of Life was cast into the lake of fire. (Revelation 20:11–15)

God's recompense is always righteous, just, impartial, and compassionate, but it will also be certain and eternal.

THE HEART OF GOD

I used to think that when God judged us, He would get some satisfaction in giving us what we rightly deserved for rejecting Him and His great love. But this is not true. God says just the opposite, in His Word.

It is *never* in the Heart (desire or will) of God that any person should come under His negative judgments and suffer the loss of His blessings. I assure you with all my heart that it is clear from God's Word that whenever God has to pronounce a negative judgment on anyone, it grieves His great, loving, gracious, tender, generous, and compassionate Heart.

When God created us, He made us, both male and female, in His own likeness and in His own image (Genesis 1:26–27). He made us with a miniature version of His great, loving nature, character, Heart, and emotions. Our human father–hearts, or mother–hearts, are tiny reflections of His Heart. When we, as loving parents, lose any of our precious children, we feel deep sorrow, agony, anguish, and loss. How *much more* must God feel this when He loses any of His dearly–loved children into a lost eternity!

Recall the Parable of the Passionate Papa. I am sure that when his younger son left him, went into a far country, and immersed himself in sinful living, the father was deeply sorrowing, painfully feeling the loss, and intensely yearning for him. When his beloved son then repented and returned, the greatness of the father's ecstatic rejoicing and celebration indicates the great degree of deep sorrow that he previously felt. This is a tiny picture of our Heavenly Father's astounding, immeasurable love for us.

A little while ago, I was in a restaurant/bar where there appeared to be quite a bit of sin and immorality going on. While I waited for my steak sandwich to be served, I said to the Lord, "You must be very grieved with all this sin." Then I heard Him say in my spirit, "All this sin doesn't grieve Me that much." Right away, I said to myself, "That must be satan talking to me, for God is a holy God." Then I heard, "No, what really grieves Me the most is their *lostness*. That is what really breaks My Heart! They are lost to Me, and I am lost to them! If they will just return to Me, I will take care of their sin, but it is their *lostness* that greatly tears My Heart!"

God's Word assures us that God is *not* at all willing that anyone should perish. He has *no* pleasure in the death of the wicked. God has done *all* that He could do to avert this, by sacrificing His Beloved Son, Jesus, on the cross.

> The Lord is not slack concerning His promise, as some count slackness, but is longsuffering toward us, not willing that any should perish but that all should come to repentance. (2 Peter 3:9)

> [God our Savior] desires all men to be saved and to come to the knowledge of the truth. For there is one God and one Mediator between God and men, the Man Christ Jesus, who gave Himself a ransom for all, to be testified in due time. (1 Timothy 2:4–6)

> Say to them: "As I live," says the Lord God, "I have no pleasure in the death of the wicked, but that the wicked turn from his way and live.

> Turn, turn from your evil ways! For why should
> you die…?" (Ezekiel 33:11)

God is infinitely and absolutely true love. This is His Heart. He wants nothing but the best and the highest good for all of us. But at the same time, God is infinitely and absolutely just. Justice must be done. God has already done everything necessary for our salvation and forgiveness by sacrificing His Son, Jesus, on the cross for all our sins.

We are the ones who make the choices now. Our choices will determine whether we will receive the positive judgments or the negative judgments.

> I call heaven and earth as witnesses today
> against you, that I have set before you life and
> death, blessing and cursing; therefore choose
> life, that both you and your descendants may
> live. (Deuteronomy 30:19)

> Therefore consider the goodness and severity
> of God: on those who fell, severity; but toward
> you, goodness, if you continue in His good-
> ness. Otherwise you also will be cut off. (Ro-
> mans 11:22)

THE FEAR OF THE LORD

The fear of the Lord is mentioned many times in Scripture. It can be greatly misunderstood. It is not a cowering, paralyzing, tormenting dread or terror. The meaning of "fear" in this context is to regard with a holy awe and reverence, to venerate and highly respect, to worship, a filial (as a child to its parents) love and obedience, to shun everything that would cause offence to the one they love.

One who "fears the Lord" reveres His holiness, loves His goodness, avoids what would displease Him, desires His favor, and stands in awe of His greatness. It is like a child who very much loves and respects his or her great big, strong, wise, loving, good, and compassionate father, and who also has a good and healthy fear of the consequences of disobeying that loving and just father.

> The fear of the Lord is the beginning of wisdom, and the knowledge of the Holy One is understanding. (Proverbs 9:10)

> The fear of the Lord is clean, enduring forever; the judgments of the Lord are true and righteous altogether. More to be desired are they than gold, yea, than much fine gold; sweeter also than honey and the honeycomb. (Psalm 19:9–10)

> But the mercy of the Lord is from everlasting to everlasting on those who fear Him, and His righteousness to children's children. (Psalm 103:17)

> Therefore, since we are receiving a kingdom which cannot be shaken, let us have grace, by which we may serve God acceptably with reverence and godly fear. For our God is a consuming fire. (Hebrews 12:28–29)

Always remember that "God is light" is completely inseparable from, and in unity and harmony with, "God is love." These two must not be separated, but must always be considered as two sides of the same coin. Each side, considered on its own without the other, will produce an unbalanced concept of the nature of God.

All of God's love is totally true, faithful, righteous, and just. All of God's light is totally loving, merciful, gracious, patient, and forgiving—beyond measure!

LET'S ASK HIM:

> God, I thank You for being a God of truth and righteousness. Please give me a heart that hungers and thirsts for Your truth and righteousness—a heart like Yours.

> Enable me to always keep Your light and Your love properly integrated together in a good, healthy balance. Don't let satan give me an unhealthy, paralyzing fear of Your justice.

> Please give me, by Your Spirit, the proper fear (awesome reverence) of You and Your Word— the good, healthy, wise, and loving fear of You.

> Help me to always remember and trust in Jesus' complete and perfect sacrifice on His cross for all my sins. Empower me to make the right choices for You.

I ask all this in the authority of my loving Creator and Redeemer, Jesus Christ.

Chapter Eleven

Express Delivery: To Everyone, With Love

God's Perfect Light for Us, in Action

One great characteristic of someone who is in love is a strong desire to communicate and express that love to the person they love. I have seen some very shy and timid people fall in love. No matter how timid they were, there developed in them a surprising and compelling desire to take the initiative and let the one they love know how much they love them.

God, the ultimate, perfect true love, is like that. He is the God who communicates and expresses Himself, His love, and His light to us, the children He so passionately loves.

Even before He created the earth, God had a part of Himself that He called "The Word," because it was His purpose to reveal Himself, to express and communicate Himself and His love to us in both words and actions—and eventually, in flesh-and-blood as a human (see John 1:1–5, 14). He named The Word "Jesus," which means "God saves."

All communication of His love to us is *always* true, faithful, righteous, and just. All communication of His truth, faithfulness, righteousness, and justice to us is *always* combined with His love, mercy, grace, longsuffering, and eagerness to forgive. These are inseparable. This combination is what God says is His wonderful goodness—His glory.

It is out of His great Heart of love that He wants to reveal His true nature, His beautiful character, His innermost being to us, His precious children. He doesn't want to keep us in the dark. He lovingly shines His light upon every one of us.

How God Reveals Himself and His Light to Us

God reveals Himself, His love, and His light to us in many ways.

His Creation

From the tiniest subatomic particles to the incomprehensible greatness of His vast universe, God reveals His greatness, power, beauty, wisdom, goodness, nature, and invisible attributes to us.

> The heavens declare the glory of God; and the firmament [expanse of sky] shows His handiwork. Day unto day utters speech, and night unto night reveals knowledge. There is no speech nor language where their voice is not heard. Their line [message] has gone out through all the earth, and their words to the end of the world. (Psalm 19:1–4)

> …because what may be known of God is manifest in them [people], for God has shown it to them. For since the creation of the world His invisible attributes are clearly seen, being un-

derstood by the things that are made, even His
eternal power and Godhead [divine nature], so
that they are without excuse. (Romans 1:19–20)

This basic knowledge of God, our Creator, is available to
us *all*, in *every* part of this planet and to *every* generation. It is
God shining His light upon us, His created children.

Our Conscience

God has created within us something called "conscience." This
is an innate (inborn) sense of what is right and what is wrong.
It is also an inner sense that there is a Supreme Being, a God,
and a need to worship Him. Our conscience is an awareness
that there is a spiritual realm as well as a physical realm.

…for when Gentiles, who do not have the law, by
nature do the things in the law, these, although
not having the law, are a law to themselves, who
show the work of the law written in their hearts,
their conscience also bearing witness, and between themselves their thoughts accusing or
else excusing them. (Romans 2:14–15)

To the pure all things are pure, but to those
who are defiled and unbelieving nothing is
pure; but even their mind and conscience are
defiled. (Titus 1:15)

This is another way that God shines His truth, righteousness, and justice into our hearts. But unfortunately, our consciences can be defiled and *"seared with a hot iron"* (1 Timothy

4:2). So we need something more sure and enduring than just our natural consciences. We need God's Spirit and His Word to really know right from wrong.

His Scriptures—The Written Word of God

God has also created humans with such an intellect that we are able to communicate to a high degree in speech and language, and He has enabled us to devise ways and means of writing these languages and thus preserve them for future generations. Read what God Himself says about His own written Word:

> The words of the LORD are pure words, like silver tried in a furnace of earth, purified seven times. You shall keep them, O LORD, You shall preserve them from this generation forever. (Psalm 12:6–7)

> The entirety of Your word is truth, and every one of Your righteous judgments endures forever. (Psalm 119:160)

> All Scripture is given by inspiration of God, and is profitable for doctrine, for reproof, for correction, for instruction in righteousness, that the man [or woman] of God may be complete, thoroughly equipped for every good work. (2 Timothy 3:16–17)

> …knowing this first, that no prophecy of Scripture is of any private interpretation, for prophecy never came by the will of man, but holy

> men of God spoke as they were moved by the
> Holy Spirit. (2 Peter 1:20–21)

> For assuredly, I [Jesus] say to you, till heaven
> and earth pass away, one jot [iota] or one tittle
> [dot] will by no means pass from the law till all
> is fulfilled. (Matthew 5:18)

So God has communicated His love, truth, righteousness, and justice to us very clearly in His Word, and has faithfully preserved His Word for us right up to this present generation. The Spirit of God takes the Word of God and makes it living and powerful to us, in us, and through us to others.

> For the word of God is living and powerful,
> and sharper than any two-edged sword, pierc-
> ing even to the division of soul and spirit, and
> of joints and marrow, and is a discerner of the
> thoughts and intents of the heart. (Hebrews
> 4:12)

> Your word I have hidden in my heart, that I
> might not sin against You. (Psalm 119:11)

His Holy Spirit

God's Spirit not only speaks to us through God's written Word, but He also speaks to us (our minds and our spirits) directly. From the creation of Adam and Eve and all the way through Scripture, there are many instances of God speaking personally to people. Occasionally, God speaks audibly, but more often He speaks in an inner voice that we can recognize as God—

sometimes gently and sometimes strongly.

Jesus, before His crucifixion and resurrection, said to His disciples, *"the Spirit of truth... dwells with you and will be in you"* (John 14:17). But after His resurrection, *"He [Jesus] breathed on them, and said to them, 'Receive the Holy Spirit'"* (John 20:22). That is when the Holy Spirit entered into the disciples and united with their spirits and they were *"born of the Spirit"* (John 3:5–8).

God prophesied in the Old Testament (Covenant) that in the New Covenant He would do this:

> I will give you a new heart and put a new spirit within you; I will take the heart of stone out of your flesh and give you a heart of flesh. I will put My Spirit within you and cause you to walk in My statutes, and you will keep My judgments and do them. (Ezekiel 36:26–27)

When anyone sincerely returns to God and by faith receives Jesus Christ as their Savior and Lord, immediately His Spirit enters and unites with their spirit (1 Corinthians 6:17 and Revelation 3:20) and they begin to be "new creations" (2 Corinthians 5:17). We then become "new men" (new selves) (Ephesians 4:22–24), which is "Christ in us" (Colossians 1:27). And His Spirit speaks to us deep inside.

God's Spirit can also speak to us through other believers, through teaching, preaching, books, recordings, personal conversations, and counseling. Also, the Holy Spirit gives various spiritual gifts to the members of the Body of Christ with which He speaks to us (1 Corinthians 12:4–11).

God's Spirit sometimes speaks to us, or through us to

others, by giving us dreams and visions (Joel 2:28 and Acts 10:9–16) or, occasionally, through angels (Acts 8:26). All these communications must be in harmony and agreement with the written Word of God and consistent with God's nature. We have an enemy who tries to deceive us. Therefore, we should ask God for His discernment and His confirmation in these things.

His Son, Jesus

But the most amazing and the most complete expression, communication, and revelation of God to us, His children, is His Son, Jesus Christ. He is called "The Word of God" (the *expression* of God) (Revelation 19:13).

> In the beginning was the Word, and the Word was with God, and the Word was God... In Him was life, and the life was the light of men... And the Word became flesh and dwelt among us, and we beheld His glory, the glory as of the only begotten of the Father, full of grace and truth. (John 1:1, 4, 14)

Jesus is the *full* revelation of both "God is love" and "God is light"—the *complete* expression of God's great, wonderful Father–Heart.

> For in Him dwells all the fullness of the Godhead [divine nature] bodily; and you are complete in Him, who is the head of all principality and power. (Colossians 2:9–10)

Jesus—His total life, character, attitude, actions, teachings, crucifixion, redemption, resurrection, and ascension—is the most explicit and vivid demonstration of God's genuine Heart and nature.

Jesus is
the ultimate
audio–visual,
stereophonic,
three–dimensional,
living color,
real–life,
flesh and blood,
in–person revelation…

…of the eternal, almighty, supreme, invisible Creator-God—our Heavenly Father.

Jesus said, *"And he who sees Me sees Him who sent Me. I have come as a light into the world, that whoever believes in Me should not abide in darkness"* (John 12:45–46).

LET'S ASK HIM:

God, thank You for being a Father who communicates and reveals Yourself to us. Reveal Yourself and Your light to me through the incredible beauty and design of Your great creation. Fill me with awe and wonder.

And God, please make my conscience much more alive and sensitive to what is really right and wrong—by Your Holy Spirit and by Your Word.

Enable me to open my heart wide to the voice of Your Spirit, and to recognize Your voice whenever You speak to me in various ways.

Make Your Scriptures come alive to me and speak to me through them.

Open wide my spiritual eyes to see Your fullness and Your wonderful Father–Heart in Jesus, Your Son.

I ask and trust You to do this, in the name of Jesus Christ, my Savior.

CHAPTER TWELVE

DOES GOD EVER LOSE HIS TEMPER?

What About God's Anger?

No! God does not ever lose His cool, lose His temper, or lose control of His emotions or His actions. If He did, I believe all of us would have been "ash in a flash" a long time ago.

God is always unchanging, always faithful, and always in control. He is always loving, as well as always being righteous and just.

But God does have righteous displeasure, indignation, and anger over untruth, unfaithfulness, unrighteousness, and injustice. His very nature is passionate for truth, faithfulness, righteousness, and justice, as well as for love, mercy, grace, longsuffering, and forgiveness. These two facets of His character are *always* perfectly integrated.

It is because God loves us so greatly and so deeply, and because His Heart so intensely desires us to be in close, loving harmony with Him, that our selfishness, indifference, disobedience, and rebellion hurts, disappoints, grieves, and offends His great loving Heart. It is because He loves us so much, not because He is nasty or harsh. Satan will try to twist this, so be careful. Even if we hurt and anger Him, God will still love us.

Well Then, What About God's Anger?

God does *not* get angry quickly. He is very patient and very longsuffering—"abundant in mercy and truth."

> But You, O Lord, are a God full of compassion, and gracious, longsuffering and abundant in mercy and truth. (Psalm 86:15)

> For His anger is but for a moment, His favor is for life; weeping may endure for a night, but joy comes in the morning. (Psalm 30:5)

God is *slow to anger*—"abounding in mercy." He will correct, reprove, and warn us, and give us time and opportunity to repent of our unrighteousness and return to Him.

> The Lord is merciful and gracious, slow to anger, and abounding in mercy. He will not always strive with us, nor will He keep His anger forever. (Psalm 103:8–9)

> Who is a God like You, pardoning iniquity and passing over the transgression of the remnant of His heritage [people]? He does not retain His anger forever, because He delights in mercy. (Micah 7:18)

Continued stubborn disobedience and deliberate rebellion on our part eventually begin to kindle God's anger. But God will still truly love us and passionately want us to return to Him.

For example, the Israelites provoked God continually in the wilderness of Sinai for forty years, to the point that *"the anger of the* Lord *was greatly aroused"* (Numbers 11:10). And eventually *"the fierce anger of the* Lord*"* was kindled (Numbers 25:4). But He did not lose His cool. This fierce anger was not because God is cruel, mean, cranky, irritable, or nasty or because He has an uncontrollable temper. It was because His people continually, again and again, rebelled, disobeyed, and hardened their hearts against Him. This violated His sense of righteousness and justice.

But God still loved them. They were still His people and He still kept His covenant with them. He still had mercy, grace, and forgiveness for them. He still fed them, led them, and protected them during those forty years. But they kept refusing Him and kept turning away from Him and His commandments—and thus kindled His anger.

He had to chastise them again and again—not to destroy them or to make them pay for their sin, but to purify them and turn them back to His righteous ways. He still called them His people, but He could not sanction or bless their disobedience and rebellion. He had to deal with it.

For example, consider parents who have righteous values and who love their children very, very much. They will likely become rightfully hurt, grieved, and eventually angered if their children continually and stubbornly disobey and rebel. But their anger does not mean they cease loving their precious children. They know that disobedience and rebellion are wrong, immoral, and injurious to their children, but they *still* love their children, deeply cherish them, and work for the highest good and greatest benefit of these whom they love so much. Because of this, they will have to lovingly deal with the disobedience and rebellion.

AN IMPORTANT WARNING

God says, *"Do not be deceived, God is not mocked; for whatever a man [or woman] sows, that he will also reap"* (Galatians 6:7).

> God's love spurned,
>   His mercy despised,
>   His grace neglected,
>   His reproofs unheeded,
>   His patience ignored,
>   His forgiveness refused,
>   His goodness abused, and
>   His chastening resisted...

progressively causes:

> God's disappointment,
>   His displeasure,
>   His hurt,
>   His offence,
>   His anger,
>   His wrath,
>   His indignation, and
>   His judgments.

But *He will still love you* and want you to repent and come back to Him.

> And you have forgotten the exhortation which speaks to you as to sons: "My son, do not despise the chastening of the LORD, nor be discouraged when you are rebuked by Him; for whom the LORD loves He chastens, and scourg-

es [disciplines] every son whom He receives."
(Hebrews 12:5–6)

As many as I love, I rebuke and chasten. Therefore be zealous and repent. (Revelation 3:19)

LET'S ASK HIM:

God, I'm very grateful that You are so patient
and longsuffering toward me, and that You
never lose Your temper.

I admit that my old human nature is prone to
selfishness and disobedience, so by the power
of Your Holy Spirit within me, keep me from
rebelling and angering You or despising Your
great mercy.

Create in me a heart that wants to obey You
and please You. Help me to repent quickly,
whenever I do sin.

Enable me to keep believing in your mercy,
Your patience, Your forgiveness, and Your true
love, even when You have to correct me. Here I
am, Lord. Do in me what I need the most.

I humbly ask You to do this, by the power of
Jesus' resurrection.

CHAPTER THIRTEEN

MERCY AND JUSTICE HAVE KISSED EACH OTHER

Mercy's Total Triumph—For Us

TWO SEEMING OPPOSITES

Justice cries out, "Sin, disobedience, and rebellion must be punished. Wrong must reap its just consequences. Retribution must be made. The guilty must be condemned."

But Mercy cries out, "Forgive the guilty; pardon all the sin, disobedience, and rebellion. Do not give the sinners what they rightly deserve. Have pity, have compassion; withdraw the condemnation. Let them go free."

God's Light cries out, "Truth, faithfulness, and righteousness have been violated. Sin must reap its wages. Disobedience and rebellion must be punished. It is not right and just to let the guilty go free without giving them all that they truly deserve. Justice must be done."

But God's great burning, passionate Love cries out, "Have mercy. Give grace. Forgive the rebel. Pardon the guilty. Let the sinner go free. Don't give condemnation. Pronounce them just and righteous. I love them passionately. I want them reconciled to me. I don't want them to perish. I yearn for them to be close to Me forever."

THE AGONIZING DILEMMA

So, God's love and light are crying out opposite demands. On the one hand, justice must be done. On the other hand, God greatly desires to pardon and forgive us. How can these seemingly opposite facets of God's perfect nature be completely reconciled with each other, and both be totally fulfilled and fully satisfied? How can mercy triumph?

God is not a split personality. He does not swing back and forth from one attitude to another. He is always, constantly, totally love and totally light integrated together. But how can He justly forgive us, His sinning children, without violating justice? How can both mercy and justice be fully accomplished at the same time?

GOD'S MARVELOUS ANSWER

God's loving, wonderful, astounding answer, His amazing, stunning solution to this dilemma is twofold: God became flesh (Jesus) and dwelt among us, and Jesus took our sin on Himself.

God Became Flesh and Dwelt Among Us

In the beginning was the Word, and the Word was with God, and the Word was God. (John 1:1)

And the Word [Jesus Christ] became flesh and dwelt among us, and we beheld His glory, the glory as of the only begotten of the Father, full of grace and truth. (John 1:14)

His eyes were like a flame of fire, and on His head were many crowns. He [Jesus] had a name written that no one knew except Himself. He was clothed with a robe dipped in blood, and His name is called The Word of God. (Revelation 19:12–13)

And without controversy great is the mystery of godliness: God was manifested in the flesh, justified in [authenticated by] the Spirit, seen by angels [the messengers], preached among the Gentiles, believed on in the world, received up in glory. (1 Timothy 3:16)

…Christ Jesus, who, being in the form of God, did not consider it robbery to be equal with God, but made Himself of no reputation, taking the form of a bondservant [slave], and coming in the likeness of men. (Philippians 2:5–7)

The Sinless Son of God Took Our Sin on Himself

Why did God become a man? So that Jesus, as both the sinless Son of Man and the Son of God, could take on Himself, on His cross, the sin of every person: our guilt, our condemnation, our death, our punishment, and our hell. Jesus willingly took our place by sacrificing Himself on our behalf as the complete, eternal sacrifice and atonement (payment) for all our sins so that we could be rightly and justly forgiven, justified, and reconciled with God, our incredibly loving, grace–filled Father. Look at what Scripture says:

And being found in appearance as a man, He humbled Himself and became obedient to the point of death, even the death of the cross. (Philippians 2:8)

But He was wounded for our transgressions, He was bruised for our iniquities; the chastisement for our peace was upon Him, and by His stripes we are healed. All we like sheep have gone astray; we have turned, every one, to his own way; and the LORD has laid on Him [Jesus] the iniquity of us all. (Isaiah 53:5–6)

For Christ also suffered once for sins, the just for the unjust, that He might bring us to God, being put to death in the flesh but made alive by the Spirit. (1 Peter 3:18)

"Who committed no sin, nor was deceit found in His mouth"; who, when He was reviled, did not revile in return; when He suffered, He did not threaten, but committed Himself to Him who judges righteously; who Himself bore our sins in His own body on the tree [cross], that we, having died to sins, might live for righteousness—by whose stripes you were healed. (1 Peter 2:22–24)

For He [God] made Him [Jesus] who knew no sin to be sin for us, that we might become the righteousness of God in Him. (2 Corinthians 5:21)

> In Him we have redemption through His
> blood, the forgiveness of sins, according to the
> riches of His grace which He made to abound
> toward us in all wisdom and prudence [under-
> standing]. (Ephesians 1:7–8)

> And He Himself is the propitiation [payment]
> for our sins, and not for ours only but also for
> the whole world. (1 John 2:2)

> …God was in Christ reconciling the world to
> Himself, not imputing [attributing, crediting]
> their trespasses to them, and has committed to
> us the word of reconciliation. (2 Corinthians
> 5:19)

God in His foreknowledge planned this salvation from
"the foundation of the world" (Revelation 13:8) and prophesied
it in detail through many of His prophets hundreds of years
before Jesus came and died for our forgiveness and our salvation. God desires and loves us so very much that He chose,
planned, and then did all this to His own dear Son in order
to rescue us from a lost eternity and win us back to His great
loving arms.

Look at Jesus on that Cruel, Cruel Cross

This is where God's mercy and justice met, embraced, kissed
each other, and were both totally fulfilled.

> Mercy and truth have met together; righteousness and peace have kissed [each other]. (Psalm 85:10)

> But You, O Lord, are a God full of compassion, and gracious, longsuffering and abundant in mercy and truth. (Psalm 86:15)

During the whole of Jesus' crucifixion—throughout the betrayal, the rejection, the humiliation, the beating, the whipping, the mocking, the crown of thorns, the nails in His hands and feet, and the six long torturous hours on that cross—Jesus was taking onto His body all our sin, our guilt, our condemnation, and our judgment. He was paying for it *all*. Yes, He who had no sin paid for *all* my sin, *all* your sin, and *all* the sins of His whole human race.

And at the end of those six long, torturous hours, Jesus shouted, *"My God, my God, why have You forsaken Me?"* (Mark 15:34). This is when the Father *"laid on Him the iniquity of us all"* (Isaiah 53:6) and began to *"make His soul an offering for sin"* (Isaiah 53:10). This is why God had to turn away from Him. Then, *"[Jesus] said, 'It is finished!' And bowing His head, He gave up His spirit"* (John 19:30). He died, guilty and condemned on our behalf, for all our sin—yours and mine.

Then, while His battered, pierced body lay for three days and three nights in that cold, dark tomb, Jesus' soul was paying for our sins in the unimaginable spiritual horror of the depths of hell.

> For David says concerning Him [Jesus]: "I foresaw the LORD always before my face, for He is at my right hand, that I may not be shaken. Therefore my heart rejoiced, and my tongue was glad; moreover my flesh [body] also will rest in hope. For You will not leave my soul in Hades [hell], nor will You allow Your Holy One to see corruption..." Therefore, being a prophet, and knowing that God had sworn with an oath to him [David] that of the fruit of his body, according to the flesh, He would raise up the Christ [Messiah] to sit on his throne, he [David], foreseeing this, spoke concerning the resurrection of the Christ, that His soul was not left in Hades [hell], nor did His flesh [body] see corruption. (Acts 2:25–27, 30–31)

> (Now this, "He ascended"—what does it mean but that He also first descended into the lower parts of the earth [hell]? He who descended is also the One who ascended far above all the heavens, that He might fill all things.) (Ephesians 4:9–10)

Then, at the end of those three days, God raised Jesus from the dead and exalted Him to His throne in heaven, far above all power and authority, demonstrating that sin had indeed been fully atoned for, and that satan, death, and hell had been forever conquered.

MERCY AND JUSTICE—BOTH TOTALLY
FULFILLED AND SATISFIED

The ultimate point where the love of God and the justice of God meet and are both completely fulfilled and satisfied is at the crucifixion, burial, and resurrection of Jesus. Now God can truthfully, faithfully, righteously, and justly forgive all who turn [repent] and come to Him by believing in and receiving Jesus as their Savior and Lord, and by receiving His death and resurrection for their salvation. God's mercy, grace, and forgiveness are now freely offered to every one of us. God makes it very clear in His Word:

> But what does it [faith] say? "The word is near you, in your mouth and in your heart" (that is, the word of faith which we preach): that if you confess with your mouth the Lord Jesus and believe in your heart that God has raised Him from the dead, you will be saved. For with the heart one believes unto righteousness, and with the mouth confession is made unto salvation. (Romans 10:8–10)

> If we confess our sins [express repentance], He is faithful and just to forgive us our sins and to cleanse us from all unrighteousness. (1 John 1:9)

> But as many as received Him, to them He gave the right to become children of God, to those who believe in His name: who were born, not of blood, nor of the will of the flesh, nor of the will of man, but of God. (John 1:12–13)

God can now righteously and justly declare us "justified" (acquitted, no longer declared guilty) and He now imputes (attributes, accredits) to us Jesus' pure, perfect righteousness even though we are completely unworthy. What an incredible exchange! Jesus takes our sin and then gives us His righteousness. How great and how wonderful is God's goodness and true love toward us! Also, His justice has been fully accomplished. Look at what God says:

> [Faith] was accounted to him [Abraham] for righteousness." Now it was not written for his sake alone that it was imputed to him, but also for us. It shall be imputed to us who believe in Him who raised up Jesus our Lord from the dead, who was delivered up [to death] because of our offenses, and was raised because of our justification. Therefore, having been justified by faith, we have peace with God through our Lord Jesus Christ, through whom also we have access by faith into this grace in which we stand, and rejoice in hope of the glory of God. (Romans 4:22–5:2)

> But God demonstrates His own love toward us, in that while we were still sinners, Christ died for us. Much more then, having now been justified by His blood, we shall be saved from wrath through Him. (Romans 5:8–9)

> There is therefore now no condemnation to those who are in Christ Jesus, who do not walk

according to the flesh, but according to the Spirit. (Romans 8:1)

MERCY TRIUMPHS OVER JUDGMENT

…Mercy triumphs over judgment. (James 2:13)

Oh, give thanks to the LORD, for He is good! For His mercy endures forever. (Psalm 107:1)

…that Christ may dwell in your hearts through faith; that you, being rooted and grounded in love, may be able to comprehend with all the saints what is the width and length and depth and height—to know the love of Christ which passes knowledge; that you may be filled with all the fullness of God. (Ephesians 3:17–19)

God wants us all to comprehend (or at least begin to comprehend) the *agape* love of Jesus Christ, which surpasses human comprehension. In the above Scripture, God mentions "the width and length" (the horizontal dimension) and then "the depth and height" (the vertical dimension) of His amazing, sacrificial, true love which is far beyond measure.

I wonder if by this God is picturing the horizontal and vertical aspects uniting, being nailed together through the hands and feet of Jesus our Savior, *forming the image of His cross.* Mercy nailed together with judgment, and triumphing over it—for us all.

BUT...

But if a person rejects God's great salvation, which is Jesus' full payment for their sins, or if they just neglect to receive *"so great a salvation"* (Hebrews 2:3), they themselves will have to pay for their own sins for eternity. What a horrible tragedy that would be, since Jesus' payment for their sins would then be in vain. That would certainly be their own choice, but definitely not God's.

> Or do you despise the riches of His goodness, forbearance, and longsuffering, not knowing that the goodness of God leads you to repentance? But in accordance with your hardness and your impenitent heart you are treasuring up for yourself wrath in the day of wrath and revelation of the righteous judgment of God, who "will render to each one according to his deeds." (Romans 2:4–6)

> For God so loved the world that He gave His only begotten Son [Jesus], that whoever believes in Him should not perish but have everlasting life. For God did not send His Son into the world to condemn the world, but that the world through Him might be saved. He who believes in Him [Jesus] is not condemned; but he who does not believe is condemned already, because he has not believed in the name of the only begotten Son of God. (John 3:16–18)

Therefore we must give the more earnest heed to the things we have heard, lest we drift away. For if the word spoken through angels proved steadfast, and every transgression and disobedience received a just reward, how shall we escape if we neglect so great a salvation, which at the first began to be spoken by the Lord [Jesus], and was confirmed to us by those who heard Him, God also bearing witness both with signs and wonders, with various miracles, and gifts of the Holy Spirit, according to His own will? (Hebrews 2:1–4)

See that you do not refuse Him who speaks. For if they did not escape who refused Him who spoke on earth, much more shall we not escape if we turn away from Him who speaks from heaven. (Hebrews 12:25)

And I saw the dead, small and great, standing before God, and books were opened. And another book was opened, which is the Book of Life. And the dead were judged according to their works, by the things which were written in the books... Then Death and Hades [hell] were cast into the lake of fire. This is the second death. And anyone not found written in the Book of Life was cast into the lake of fire. (Revelation 20:12, 14–15)

LET'S ASK HIM:

Thank You, thank You, thank You, Father, for Your incredible love, mercy, and grace that have triumphed over all the judgment that I deserve for all my sin.

Thank You forever, Jesus, for coming in the flesh to atone for all my sins by Your agonizing crucifixion.

Ten thousand thanks to You for taking onto Yourself all our sin, guilt, condemnation, and hell, and then imputing to us Your perfect, pure righteousness and forgiveness.

Heavenly Father, please give me an undying faith and gratitude for Your victorious, great, loving, forgiving Father–Heart.

Do this, for Your glory and praise, in Jesus' wonderful, victorious name.

CHAPTER FOURTEEN

GOD'S GREAT, ASTOUNDING LOVE

Nailed to a Cruel, But Conquering Cross

This chapter is in a different format. It's what I call "power poetry." It is not meant to be pleasing entertainment, but a strong, fervent message of God's great love for us—and of our love and gratitude back to Him.

This was given to me by God, bit by bit, over many months, very much to my surprise. Then, in an amazing way, He clearly indicated that it should be a part of this book. Every bit of it is based on God's Scriptures.

This poem portrays us, you and me, speaking directly and personally from our own hearts to Jesus and to our great, loving Father. It is our love–gift to Them, for Their amazing love–gift to us.

GOD'S GREAT, ASTOUNDING LOVE— NAILED TO A CRUEL, BUT CONQUERING CROSS

Jesus, You Gave Yourself—for Us

Jesus, You are the Only Begotten Son of God,
Full of God's boundless love, grace, and truth.
Truly You are God Manifest in the Flesh for me
—and for Your whole, dark, sinful, lost world!

Jesus, all of God's glory shone from Your sinless life,
And Your crucifixion was God's astounding sacrifice,
To give His white–hot burning Love to us all!

You were betrayed, denied, and utterly forsaken,
Spit on, brutally bruised, and cruelly beaten,
Rejected, slandered, condemned, and crucified,
Yes, for me—and yes, for us all!
Jesus, You willingly paid the greatest price:
You were God's Great Love–Gift sacrifice,
On Your cruel, cruel cross, for us all!

You, the King of Glory, were shamed, despised,
Reviled, ridiculed, mocked, and scorned!
Willingly endured the whip, the thorns, the nails,
For me—and for us all!
Jesus, You paid the terribly painful price:
Your shed blood was God's precious sacrifice,
On Your cruel, cruel cross, for us all!

You were stripped, whipped, horribly blasphemed
And Your back was like a fresh–plowed field.
Jesus, You hung, nailed, for six long, torturous hours,
For me—and for us all!
Jesus, Your "visage was marred more than any man";
A spear pierced Your Heart, Your blood poured out,
On Your cruel, cruel cross, for us all!

Jesus, on Your cruel, cruel cross You lovingly
Bore all my awful sin and all my great guilt!

You suffered, bled, and died there—for me,
Even for me—and even for us all!
Jesus, You paid the full and complete price:
You were God's loving, ultimate sacrifice,
On Your cruel, cruel cross, for us all!

Then Your battered body lay in that dark, cold tomb,
While Your spotless soul atoned for all our sin,
Suffering unimaginable horrors in the depths of hell,
For me—and for us all!
Jesus, You paid the astounding, supreme price:
Your sinless soul was God's Burnt Sacrifice,
In the awful depths of hell, for us all!

Father, You Gave Your Son—for Us

Father, Your burning, immeasurable Love for us all
Compelled You, from the foundation of the world,
To plan and ordain all of Jesus' suffering and death,
For me—and for us all!
Father, You fully gave Yourself to us, through Him,
And Jesus took all our sin, our death, and our hell,
On His cruel cross, and in His cold tomb, for us all!

Father, You were in Your Beloved Son,
Suffering fully as much as He,
To reconcile to Yourself, Your whole lost world,
Including me—and including us all!
Jesus, alone, is The New and Living Way back into
The arms of Your astounding, eternal Father–Love,
By His cruel cross, and the depths of hell, for us all!

Father, You had to forsake Your Own Beloved Son,
When You laid our iniquity upon Your Holy One.
You made Jesus "to be sin for us" all,
Yes, for us all—including me!
Father, You paid the astounding, ultimate price:
Jesus was Your precious Love–Gift sacrifice,
On His cruel, cruel cross, for us all!

Father, the deep anguish You must have felt
To make Your Beloved Son, Jesus, suffer so,
To do all this to Your Only Begotten Son,
For me—and for us all!
Father, You paid the full atonement price:
Your Dear Son is Your supreme Love–Gift sacrifice
On His cruel—**but**—conquering cross, for us all!

Father, You Gave Jesus—for Us All

For every man and woman, and
For every boy and girl,
Of every nation, tribe, and tongue
—on all this planet earth!
Jesus, You fully paid the everlasting price:
Redemption for Your whole human race
On Your glorious, saving cross, for all the world!

You defeated satan and our sinful old–selves;
Triumphantly won the keys to death and hell,
And overcame all the darkness of Your lost world,
For me—and for us all!
Jesus, You conquered all the demonic powers

And became the King of Kings and Lord of Lords,
Through Your victorious, triumphant cross, for us all!

How extremely precious we all must be to You,
Of what high, high value and great, great worth,
For You to make such an incredible sacrifice,
For me—and, yes, for us all!
Jesus, we were all captives of sin and selfishness,
And You totally paid the immense ransom–price,
On Your redeeming, liberating cross, for us all!

Jesus, You looked ahead to totally undeserving me,
And to all who would ever believe in You.
You saw that our love would be a greatly cherished joy,
To You, Jesus—and also to You, Father,
A very precious treasure and an extreme delight,
Worth all Your wonderful, vicarious sacrifice,
On Your astounding, marvelous cross, for us all!

Jesus/Father, I Now Receive—You

Jesus/Father, I'm filled with great awe and wonder,
Totally astounded and absolutely amazed,
To see Your great, burning, eternal Love for me
—and for Your whole, dark, sinful, lost world!
Jesus, Your passionate Love has totally won my heart,
By Your atoning and substitutionary death,
On Your precious, loving cross, for us all!

Jesus, spotless Passover Lamb of God,
By faith I receive Your precious shed blood.

I receive all of Your supreme, loving sacrifice.
And You want us all—by faith, to receive You!
Jesus/Father, fervent love and gratitude fill my heart
And joyous praise overflows from my lips,
Because Your shed blood is the River of Life, for us all!

Now, by Your death, all of my sins are forgiven,
Totally blotted out, never to be remembered,
And they are all cast into the depths of the sea.
And this is for all—who humbly receive You!
Jesus, instead of all my shameful sin, You now freely
Impute to me all of Your pure righteousness,
Through Your amazing, grace–filled cross, for us all!

Now You are seated on Your throne in Heaven,
Risen, absolutely triumphant, from the dead!
You reign supreme, in all power and majesty,
Forevermore—for all who have received You!
Jesus, You live victoriously to intercede for us.
I receive, by Your grace alone, Your total victory,
Flowing from Your glorious throne, for us all!

Jesus/Father, I Now Give Myself—to You

Father, You love to choose and use
Even the foolish and the weak,
Filling and flowing out through even me,
And through all—who have received You!
Jesus, You live victoriously in my heart,
And Your Holy Spirit is now entwined with mine.
So reveal Yourself to Your lost, lost world, through me!

Jesus/Father, I completely give You all of myself,
Fervently and joyfully, as a "living sacrifice."
This is my love-gift, with deep, deep gratitude,
To You, Jesus—and also to You, Father!
I totally dedicate and submit my all to You,
And passionately apply to my whole life
Your cross! It is the **Tree of Life**, for me—
And for all who,
> By faith, sincerely
>> Receive You, Jesus,
>>> As their Savior
>>>> And as their Lord:
Total forgiveness!
> Complete acceptance!
>> Spiritual new birth!
>>> Great transformation!
>>>> And glorious eternal life!
Postscript
> …to be continued,
>> …exuberantly and passionately,
>>> …throughout all of eternity!

LET'S ASK HIM:

Father, I thank You, with all my heart, for Your astounding, white-hot burning love for me, and for sacrificing Your dear Son, Jesus, to redeem me from all my sin.

Please give me the faith to humbly receive Your great love, Your Son Jesus, and His total atonement for the forgiveness of all my sin.

Enable me to completely give myself back to You, as my love–gift, with deep, deep joyous gratitude.

Through Jesus' death and resurrection, Father, I come back into the great, big arms of Your astounding, unconditional love.

Father, hold me close to your Heart—forever!

PART THREE

The Wonderful
Father-Heart of God

CHAPTER FIFTEEN

THE FLAWLESS FATHER—FAR, FAR ABOVE ALL OTHERS

The Perfect Father-Heart—Beyond Measure

We have been learning about the great and wonderful nature of God, our eternal, all-wise, and all-powerful Creator.

If this great, holy God were a distant, aloof, uninvolved, unloving, uncaring Creator way up in the heavenly realm somewhere, then that would leave us helpless, alone, unloved, uncared for, and abandoned.

But no! Our great Creator is a loving, caring Father, right to the very core of His being. He was the Father before He created us. He is Our Father right now. He always has been and always will be our Father. God's Heart is a Father-Heart. And He does not change. He is our Heavenly Father: close, caring, tender, loving, faithful, and affectionate, involved with us and revealing Himself to us. He even came down to us, right down to our human level, to reveal Himself and His incredible, intensely-burning, immeasurable Father-Love.

Let's take a close look at what God Himself says in His Word about being a Father to us.

GOD IS ETERNALLY OUR FATHER

Even before God created us humans, He had a Father–Heart. There is some indication in Scripture that God had a Father relationship with His angels in heaven. He called His angels *"the sons of God"* (Genesis 6:1–4), and He evidently gave them free will (which is necessary for a love relationship) because some of the angels eventually chose to rebel against Him (Revelation 12:7–9).

In His foreknowledge, even before He created the earth, God chose each one of us and preplanned (predestined) us to be His sons and daughters, and to receive and freely enjoy His lavish Father–Love.

> …Blessed are You, LORD God of Israel, our Father, forever and ever. (1 Chronicles 29:10)

> …His name will be called Wonderful, Counselor, Mighty God, Everlasting Father, Prince of Peace. (Isaiah 9:6)

> …[God] has saved us and called us with a holy calling, not according to our works, but according to His own purpose and grace which was given to us in Christ Jesus before time began. (2 Timothy 1:9)

GOD DELIBERATELY CHOSE TO BE OUR FATHER

The eternal Father wanted us, chose us, and planned each one of us even before He laid the foundation of the world. We are not an accident, even if our parents may have thought so. We are not the result of millions of random accidental circumstances, as the evolutionists say. You and I are desired, designed, deliberately chosen, and decidedly loved by our great Creator–Father.

> Blessed be the God and Father of our Lord Jesus Christ, who… chose us in Him before the foundation of the world, that we should be holy and without blame before Him in love, having predestined us to adoption as sons [and daughters] by Jesus Christ to Himself, according to the good pleasure of His will. (Ephesians 1:3–5)

God Created Us to Be His Children

Then, when God created the earth, He said to Himself, *"Let Us make mankind in Our image, according to Our likeness"* (Genesis 1:26). This was His way of saying, "Let's have children." Evidently, God wanted earthly children, as well as the heavenly angels, upon whom He could lavish His great Father–Love. He created us to be like Himself, with natures like His, that need to love and be loved. This is why we exist. This is who we really are: God's love–children.

> So God created man in His own image; in the image of God He created him; male and female He created them. Then God blessed them, and God said to them, "Be fruitful and multiply; fill the earth and subdue it; have dominion over the fish of the sea, over the birds of the air, and over every living thing that moves on the

earth." (Genesis 1:27–28)

> And the LORD God formed man of the dust of
> the ground, and breathed into his nostrils the
> breath of life [His Spirit]; and man became a
> living being [soul]. (Genesis 2:7)

The Hebrew word here for "breath" also means "spirit," so God breathed His own Spirit into man's spirit. Thus, man was born physically, and also born spiritually. He was created a spirit–being living in a physical body.

So we see that God wanted a multitude of His children, in His likeness, with His nature and His Spirit within them, to fill His earth so that He could enjoy a very large family, with His great, astounding, immeasurable love.

Oops, a Disaster!

Because God is love, and because He created us to receive His love and also to love Him in return, He gave us a free will—the freedom to choose. Without a free will, we would have just been robots, not love–children. He gave His newly created son and daughter a command which they could choose to obey, or choose to disobey (Genesis 2:16–17). Eventually satan tempted them, lied to them, and deceived them into disobeying their Father's command (Genesis 3:1–6).

Thus sin entered God's human race. God's Holy Spirit, which was dwelling in their spirits (Genesis 2:7), could no longer unite with their spirits, and therefore departed from them, leaving their spirits empty, lonely, dark, and dead. At that moment, they died spiritually, even though their bodies lived for a long time afterwards. They were now alienated and separated from their loving, holy Father. Their close communion with Him was broken and they were afraid (Genesis 3:7–24).

But...

But amazingly, God still loved them and wanted to reconcile them to Himself. He prophesied to them that the Seed of the woman (Jesus Christ) would defeat satan (Genesis 3:15). God then clothed them with the skins of animals, as a prophetic picture of the shedding of Christ's blood—covering the sins of His whole human race. God then instituted a system of blood sacrifices (Genesis 4:3–5), to be made in faith, anticipating the ultimate, complete sacrifice of Jesus shedding His blood on His cross.

Straying, Lost, Lonely Children—Reconciled

God's Word says that through Adam sin entered God's whole human race, and death through sin (Romans 5:12), and that all of us have sinned and fall short of the glory of God (Romans 3:23).

> All we like sheep have gone astray; we have turned, every one, to his own way; and the LORD has laid on Him [Jesus] the iniquity of us all. (Isaiah 53:6)

> For since by man came death, by Man also came the resurrection of the dead. For as in Adam all die, even so in Christ all shall be made alive. (1 Corinthians 15:21–22)

> For if when we were enemies we were recon-
> ciled to God through the death of His Son,
> much more, having been reconciled, we shall
> be saved by His life. (Romans 5:10)

A Very Crucial Distinction: Born Physically and Born Spiritually

In the beginning, God created us humans in His likeness and in His image and with His Spirit within us, but we sinned and are now spiritually empty and dead, alienated, and separated from Him. His likeness and image in us have been badly damaged and twisted, but the potential is still there, waiting to be renewed and re-created by the victory and resurrection power of Jesus. This is why we must now be reborn spiritually.

Until each of us individually and personally turn our hearts and wills back to our loving Heavenly Father and receive Jesus' crucifixion and resurrection for our salvation, we remain straying, lost, lonely, and Fatherless. This is why Jesus told even a righteous and very religious man:

> Most assuredly, I say to you, unless one is
> born again [reborn spiritually] he cannot see
> the kingdom of God... That which is born of
> the flesh is flesh, and that which is born of the
> Spirit is spirit. Do not marvel that I said to you,
> "You must be born again." (John 3:3, 6–7)

Every human was created to be God's child, in God's image, but because of sin we all must be reborn spiritually into the Father's spiritual family by receiving Jesus as our Savior and Lord. As we just read, Jesus said very emphatically that spiritual rebirth is absolutely essential.

> But as many as received Him [Jesus], to them He gave the right to become children of God, to those who believe in His name: who were born, not of blood, nor of the will of the flesh, nor of the will of man, but of God. (John 1:12–13)

God Is Surely Our Father

A few times in the Old Testament, God referred to Himself as a Father to His chosen people, Israel. But when Jesus came, He almost always referred to God as His Father, and our Father.

> Doubtless You are our Father... You, O LORD, are our Father; our Redeemer from Everlasting is Your name. (Isaiah 63:16)

> Jesus said to her [Mary Magdalene], "...go to My brethren and say to them, 'I am ascending to My Father and your Father, and to My God and your God.'" (John 20:17)

> [Jesus said,] "In this manner, therefore, pray: Our Father in heaven, hallowed [revered] be Your name." (Matthew 6:9)

God Is Eagerly and Passionately Our Father, Our "Papa"

Look at all that God has done and the incredible price He and Jesus paid on the cross in order to redeem (save) us and receive us back into the arms of His great love again. Ponder how greatly He loved us, how intensely He desires and passionately longs for us, how great a sacrifice He made for us on the cross and in the tomb. What an amazing hunger He has for us to love Him in return, and how precious and priceless we must be to Him! He wants us to affectionately call Him "Abba," meaning "Papa" or "Daddy." Being in the arms of His great love is illustrated for us in Chapter 19.

> But when the fullness of the time had come, God sent forth His Son, born of a woman, born under the law, to redeem those who were under the law, that we might receive the adoption as sons [and daughters]. And because you are sons [and daughters], God has sent forth the Spirit of His Son into your hearts, crying out, "Abba [Papa], Father!" (Galatians 4:4–6)

> For you did not receive the spirit of bondage again to fear, but you received the Spirit of adoption by whom we cry out, "Abba [Papa], Father." The Spirit Himself bears witness with our spirit that we are children of God, and if children, then heirs—heirs of God and joint heirs with Christ, if indeed we suffer with Him, that we may also be glorified together. (Romans 8:15–17)

The very moment we return to God to follow Him, and by faith receive Jesus and His salvation (redemption), God puts the Spirit of Jesus (the Holy Spirit) into our hearts and we become born of the Spirit and new creatures in Christ—His spiritual children—and He, our spiritual Father–Papa.

> Therefore, if anyone is in Christ, he is a new creation; old things have [are] passed away; behold, all things have [are] become new. (2 Corinthians 5:17)

Jesus illustrated the eagerness and the intense love of the Father in His Parable of the Passionate Papa (see Chapter 9), otherwise known as the Parable of the Prodigal Son (Luke 15:11–32). Remember when the wayward son returned, how eagerly and passionately the father ran out to meet him, hugged and kissed him, and celebrated with a feast and with singing and dancing?

God Has Promised to Be Our Father, Our "Papa"

God has clearly declared it. It is His promise, an integral part of His New Covenant with us (Hebrews 8:10). He is faithful. He cannot break His own covenant—He will be a Father to us. We can indeed trust Him to be our true, loving Father–Papa.

> Do not be unequally yoked together with unbelievers. For what fellowship has righteousness with lawlessness? And what communion has light with darkness? And what accord has Christ with Belial [satan]? Or what part [partnership] has a believer with an unbeliever? And what agreement has the temple of God with idols? For you are the temple of the living

God. As God has said: "I will dwell in them and walk among them. I will be their God, and they shall be My people." Therefore "Come out from among them [unbelievers] and be separate, says the Lord. Do not touch what is unclean, and I will receive you. I will be a Father to you, and you shall be My sons and daughters, says the LORD Almighty." Therefore, having these promises, beloved, let us cleanse ourselves from all filthiness of the flesh and spirit, perfecting holiness in the fear of God. (2 Corinthians 6:14–7:1)

Notice in the above Scripture that God gives us a condition that we, His children, are to fulfill in order to receive and enjoy all the blessings of His wonderful Father–Heart. He says, *"Come out from among them [unbelievers] and be separate [different]… Do not touch what is unclean [filthy, lawless, dark, satanic, idolatrous]."* Only then does God say, *"I will receive you. I will be a Father to you."*

Let me illustrate this from the Parable of the Passionate Papa (Luke 15:11–32), which we looked at in Chapter 9. As long as the prodigal son was far away from his father, while he was "yoked together" with the harlots and in fellowship and partnership with unrighteousness and satan's darkness, he was not experiencing—and could not experience—the protection, provision, riches, and blessings of, and loving intimacy with, his father.

But as soon as he came to his senses, repented, and returned home, his father ran out to him, embraced him, forgave him, clothed him, cleansed him, fed him, provided for him, and greatly rejoiced. Once again, the son was enjoying the fullness of his father's great, loving heart and all the wonderful things that his father had for him.

A word of explanation is necessary here. When God says, *"Come out from among them [unbelievers] and be separate [different],"* He does *not* mean that we should pull out of our society and not associate with unbelievers. He means that we who have received Jesus and have been born again, born of the Spirit (John 3:3–8), are not to be the same as, one with, or in lifestyle–agreement with those who have not yet received Jesus as their Savior and Lord. We are now in a different family, with a different Father, and belong to a different kingdom.

> He [God] has delivered us from the power of darkness and conveyed [transferred] us into the kingdom of the Son of His love, in whom we have redemption through His blood, the forgiveness of sins. (Colossians 1:13–14)

> And you He [God] made alive, who were dead in trespasses and sins, in which you once walked according to the course of this world, according to the prince of the power of the air [satan], the spirit who now works in the sons of disobedience, among whom also we all once conducted ourselves in the lusts of our flesh, fulfilling the desires of the flesh and of the mind, and were by nature children of wrath, just as the others. (Ephesians 2:1–3)

But we are *not* to consider ourselves as superior or "better than they," nor are we to have a "holier than you" attitude. We must be beautifully humble, as Jesus was.

We are to be different and live differently, but we, like Jesus, are to love them, befriend them, pray for them, and be a witness to them of Christ and His wonderful salvation. Jesus prayed for us, His disciples, in this manner:

> I do not pray that You [Father] should take them out of the world, but that You should keep them from the evil one. They are not of the world, just as I am not of the world. Sanctify them [set them apart] by Your truth. Your word is truth. As You sent Me into the world, I also have sent them into the world. (John 17:15–18)

Jesus is our great example. He loved the sinful and unbelieving (as well as the righteous and religious). He spent time with them, went into their homes, and ate with them. He had compassion on them. He told them about the Father's great love, mercy, and forgiveness. He talked to them about the ways of righteousness and about returning to God. But Jesus was sharply criticized for this by the hypocritical, super–strict, harsh, proud, and legalistic religious leaders. They accused Him of being *"a friend of tax collectors [swindlers] and sinners"* (Luke 7:34).

> Then all the tax collectors and the sinners drew near to Him to hear Him. And the Pharisees and scribes complained, saying, "This Man receives [welcomes] sinners and eats with them." (Luke 15:1–2)

This was why Jesus gave them the parables of the lost sheep, the lost coin, and the lost son (the Parable of the Passionate Papa) in Luke 15:3–32.

Yes, Jesus loved the sinners, befriended them, and socialized with them, but He never compromised righteousness nor defiled Himself. And He led many of them back to God. We should do likewise. This is the Father's true Heart of love, compassion, and humility.

GOD IS OUR GOOD AND PERFECT FATHER, OUR "PAPA"

Remember when God revealed His goodness to Moses on Mount Sinai (Exodus 34:5–7)? (See Chapter 2.) His goodness was an integration of mercy, grace, and forgiveness along with truth, faithfulness, righteousness, and justice. So our Father is the absolute, true, eternal, totally good, benevolent, beneficent, generous, compassionate, gracious, and perfect true-love Father.

> Oh, how great is Your goodness, which You have laid up for those who fear [revere] You, which You have prepared for those who trust in You… (Psalm 31:19)

I use the word "perfect" because Jesus called the Father "holy" (John 17:11) and "holy" means total perfection and perfect totality—absolutely flawless. (See Chapter 5.)

> Holy, holy, holy, Lord God Almighty, Who was and is and is to come! (Revelation 4:8)

God will be a totally good, loving, and perfect Father–Papa to us. He cannot be anything less, because this is the very essence of His eternal character and nature.

Unfortunately, the word "father" evokes in many people a bad connotation—and with some people, even horrible memories—due to character failures, lack of love and affection, harshness, neglect, cruelty, rejection, or even awful abuses that they experienced from their earthly fathers.

The devil works overtime to corrupt fathers and mothers, to twist them, to bend them out of shape, to pervert them, to make them exactly the opposite of what God is genuinely like, so that there will be whole generations that grow up thinking, "If that's God, who wants him? If that's what He is like, no thanks!"

To the degree that our earthly fathers and mothers portrayed a distorted role model of God to us, we will likely have a distorted concept of, a wrong fear of, or even a strong aversion to God, our Heavenly Father.

Even though the devil has done all that twisting and distorting, the grace of God has a remedy for it. God *can* straighten out the bent, twisted, perverted concepts we have of "father." The Word of God *can* pierce the darkness, turn on the light, and expose the lies, deceptions, and slanders. We *can* begin to see what our Heavenly Father is truly like—not the way we were brought up to think of "father." God's Spirit *can* do this. Jesus *can* heal—not only our bodies, but more importantly He *can* also heal our minds, our spirits, our souls, our emotions, our wounds, and our hurts. He *can* heal our memories and our past. This is not too hard for Him. Jesus very much wants to show the beautiful and perfect Father to us, and for us to enjoy

Him greatly and eternally.

Yes, God is truly our good, loving, and perfect Papa. He wants us to believe this, know this, experience this, and enjoy Him forever. He Himself has said this to us, His children, again and again through His Scriptures, and He wants to prove it to us personally and experientially.

LET'S ASK HIM:

> God, I want to really believe in and receive You as my great, big, loving Heavenly Father.
>
> Help me to believe all that You have written in Your Word about You being my perfect Heavenly Papa.
>
> Give me a strong, unshakable faith in You as my eternal Daddy. I eagerly want to experience a real, ever-growing, intimate, personal love-relationship with You.
>
> Please heal in me every disappointment, every distortion, every hurt or wound, and every abuse or twisted concept of fatherhood that I may have ever received.
>
> Deliver me from any fear or aversion that I may have so that I can open my heart wide to You and give myself into Your great, totally loving, everlasting arms as Your very own child.
>
> Papa, here I am. Pick me up, hug me, and hold me close. In Jesus' name.

CHAPTER SIXTEEN

EXPRESS DELIVERY: FOR ALL HIS CHILDREN

God's Perfect Father–Love For Us, in Action

A VERY SPECIAL RELATIONSHIP

The kind of person God eternally is will be the kind of Father He eternally will be to us. In Parts 1 and 2 of this book, we began to see the wonderful nature, character, disposition, and Heart of God—the very deep, everlasting, unchanging essence and core of His being. God brings into His Fatherhood all of His beautiful, perfect, loving, and righteous nature. He cannot be anything less, as our Father. But in His Father–relationship with us, these wonderful attributes are greatly focused and intensified towards us, because we have become His very own spiritual sons and daughters.

Now, in Part 3, we begin to see the very special way that He focuses all of His great Father goodness, love, and faithfulness on us, His own spiritual children, we who have sincerely turned back to Him and have by faith personally received the crucified and resurrected Jesus as our Savior and Lord. By receiving Christ, we have been born again, born of the Spirit, into God's great family.

Let me illustrate why this Father–child relationship is a very special and intense application of God's great and loving Heart.

Consider an unmarried man who is, by nature, a very loving, kind, gentle, generous, compassionate, tender, and righteous person. He loves and enjoys children and relates with them very, very well. When he marries and has a child of his own, all of his wonderful character and nature is now, in a very special way, centered on and expressed to his own child, in a much greater fervor, passion, and delight than his general love for all other children. This is his own, precious child—in his own image and in his own likeness.

I can still well remember the first time I held my first child in my arms. My wife handed her to me. My tiny daughter was wrapped up tight in a blanket. I held her in my arms and, after a few seconds, she moved and squirmed. The thoughts raced through my mind, *She's mine! She's my very own child! This is utterly thrilling!* Something happened in me at that moment that has never gone away. I had held babies before and played with young children, but this was far beyond anything I had ever experienced. God created fathers and mothers to be like that, because that is the way He is, deep within His wonderful Father–Heart, toward us, His very own spiritual sons and daughters.

JUST BY BEING BORN INTO HIS FAMILY

All the special manifestations of God's perfect Father–Heart and all the wonderful expressions of His great Father–love are ours, just by being born into His family. They cannot be earned, worked for, or deserved—just like a newborn earthly baby cannot do anything to merit being accepted, loved, adored, and cherished by his or her parents. A child is totally loved and cared for, just because it is the precious child of its parents. And so it is, even more so, with God and us, His children. All we need to do is freely receive and enjoy all His love and care. He is truly our great, big, loving, Heavenly Papa.

THE EXPRESSION OF GOD'S GREAT, PERFECT FATHER-HEART

This is how God's great, perfect Father–Heart is expressed to us: through the love, mercy, provision, protection, fairness, delight, inheritance, instruction, and correction He gives us.

Perfect Father Love

God's *agape* love (see Chapters 8 and 9) is especially focused on and intensely expressed to us, His children.

> Behold what manner of love the Father has bestowed on us, that we should be called children of God! (1 John 3:1)

Jesus said this amazing thing about His disciples:

> I in them, and You in Me; that they may be made perfect in one, and that the world may know that You have sent Me, and have loved them as You have loved Me… And I have declared to them Your name, and will declare it, that the love with which You loved Me may be in them, and I in them. (John 17:23, 26)

Jesus says here that the Father loves us just like He loves Jesus. This is astounding! It is beyond our comprehension, but it is true. He is our Abba, our Papa, just like He is to Jesus.

> Jesus answered and said to him, "If anyone loves Me, he will keep My word; and My Father will love him, and We will come to him and make Our home with him." (John 14:23)

Perfect Father Mercy

"Mercy" means *not* getting the punishment we deserve, but *instead* getting the favor (grace) we don't deserve. The Hebrew word for "mercy" also includes the concept of grace, loving-kindness, pity, compassion, tenderness, patience, and forgiveness. Our Papa–God is just like that!

> Blessed be the God and Father of our Lord Jesus Christ, the Father of mercies and God of all comfort [encouragement, strengthening], who comforts us in all our tribulation, that we may be able to comfort those who are in any trouble, with the comfort with which we ourselves are comforted by God. (2 Corinthians 1:3–4)

> And the Word [Jesus] became flesh and dwelt among us, and we beheld His glory, the glory as of the only begotten of the Father, full of grace and truth. (John 1:14)

> As a father pities his children, so the LORD pities those who fear [revere] Him. For He knows

our frame; He remembers that we are dust.
(Psalm 103:13–14)

As one whom his mother comforts [strength-
ens, encourages], so I will comfort you; and
you shall be comforted… (Isaiah 66:13)

Remember the Parable of the Passionate Papa? Jesus uses
this parable to illustrate for us the great merciful Father–Heart
and the forgiveness of God for His straying, sinning children
who return to Him (Luke 15:20–24).

Perfect Father Provision

God is totally and eternally good. He is lovingly kind and generous, especially to His own children. He most certainly is not
miserly, mean, or stingy. He delights in giving us good things.
It is always by His great loving grace. We cannot ever deserve
this or earn it. It is just because we are His precious, cherished
children, born of His Spirit.

But He does not give us everything we selfishly or foolish-
ly want or ask for. He loves us too much to do that. God's *agape*
love is always determined to work for our highest and greatest
good, both for the here–and–now and especially for eternity.
He does this for us, even more often than a good, loving, and
wise earthly parent will sometimes say "No" to the foolish, detrimental, or dangerous requests of his or her beloved child.

…For your Father knows the things you have
need of before you ask Him. (Matthew 6:8)

> If you then, being evil, know how to give good gifts to your children, how much more will your Father who is in heaven give good things to those who ask Him! (Matthew 7:11)

> Every good gift and every perfect gift is from above, and comes down from the Father of lights, with whom there is no variation or shadow [hint] of turning [changing]. (James 1:17)

> And my God shall supply all your need according to His riches in glory by Christ Jesus. (Philippians 4:19)

Perfect Father Protection

We are God's extremely precious little children and He has promised again and again to protect us. In the Scriptures, for example, He promises to be our shield, our strong tower, our deliverer, our fortress, and our shepherd. It is wonderful to have a great, big, all-powerful, loving, caring Heavenly Papa to look after us like this.

> The LORD is my strength and my shield; my heart trusted in Him, and I am helped... (Psalm 28:7)

> The eternal God is your refuge, and underneath are the everlasting arms; He will thrust out the enemy from before you, and will say, "Destroy!" (Deuteronomy 33:27)

Are not two sparrows sold for a copper coin? And not one of them falls to the ground apart from your Father's will. But the very hairs of your head are all numbered. Do not fear therefore; you are of more value than many sparrows. (Matthew 10:29–31)

Take heed that you do not despise one of these little ones [children], for I say to you that in heaven their angels always see the face of My Father who is in heaven. (Matthew 18:10)

My Father, who has given them to Me [Jesus], is greater than all; and no one is able to snatch them out of My Father's hand. I and My Father are one. (John 10:29–30)

Perfect Father Fairness

God's inner nature is total, perfect love, and His love is perfectly true, faithful, righteous, and just. He loves every one of His children equally, totally, and without favoritism. He created us all different, and He has different plans for each of us, and we all respond to Him differently. But His love for each of us is the same: total, constant, and without partiality. He loves every one of us equally.

For there is no partiality with God. (Romans 2:11)

For the LORD your God is God of gods and Lord of lords, the great God, mighty and awesome, who shows no partiality nor takes a bribe. (Deuteronomy 10:17)

...the Father, who without partiality judges according to each one's work... (1 Peter 1:17)

Then Peter opened his mouth and said: "In truth I perceive that God shows no partiality. But in every nation whoever fears [reveres] Him and works righteousness is accepted by Him." (Acts 10:34–35)

The LORD is good to all, and His tender mercies are over all His works. (Psalm 145:9)

Perfect Father Delight

The word "delight" is a strong word meaning great, intense enjoyment and pleasure. Even though we all, to varying degrees, are immature, foolish, failing little children, God delights in us. Have you ever seen loving, caring parents greatly enjoying and delighting in their babies and in their very young children? It is beautiful to watch.

...looking unto Jesus, the author and finisher of our faith, who for the joy [delight] that was set before Him [us and our love for Him] endured the cross, despising the shame, and has sat down at the right hand of the throne of God. (Hebrews 12:2)

You shall no longer be termed Forsaken, nor shall your land any more be termed Desolate;

but you shall be called Hephzibah [My De-
light], and your land Beulah [Married]; for the
LORD delights in you... and as the bridegroom
rejoices over the bride, so shall your God rejoice over you. (Isaiah 62:4–5)

The LORD your God in your midst, the Mighty
One, will save; He will rejoice over you with
gladness, He will quiet you with His love, He will
rejoice over you with singing. (Zephaniah 3:17)

For whom the LORD loves He corrects, just as
a father the son [or daughter] in whom he delights. (Proverbs 3:12)

This is mind–boggling! It is the greatness of His intense
Father–Love for us all that causes Him such great delight in us,
in spite of all our faults, failures, sins, and weaknesses.

Perfect Father Inheritance

The very moment we give ourselves back to God and receive
Jesus, we are born again by the Spirit of God into His spiritual
family. Unworthy as we all are, by His grace we become His
heirs just by being born again, from above.

The Spirit Himself bears witness with our spirit
that we are children of God, and if children, then
heirs—heirs of God and joint heirs with Christ,
if indeed we suffer with Him, that we may also
be glorified together. (Romans 8:16–17)

> Blessed be the God and Father of our Lord Jesus Christ, who according to His abundant mercy has begotten [birthed] us again to a living hope through the resurrection of Jesus Christ from the dead, to an inheritance incorruptible and undefiled and that does not fade away, reserved in heaven for you, who are kept by the power of God through faith for salvation ready to be revealed in the last time. (1 Peter 1:3–5)

> O LORD, You are the portion of my inheritance and my cup; You maintain my lot [share]…Yes, I have a good inheritance. (Psalm 16:5–6)

Perfect Father Instruction

As a perfect loving Father, God is always working for our highest benefit and our greatest good. So He is progressively and continually teaching and training us, developing and maturing us, purifying and correcting us. He is transforming us into the beautiful image of His Son, Jesus Christ, so that the people around us may see Him and His great love for them.

> But we all, with unveiled face, beholding as in a mirror the glory of the Lord, are being transformed into the same image from glory to glory, just as by the Spirit of the Lord. (2 Corinthians 3:18)

> All Scripture is given by inspiration of God, and is profitable for doctrine [teaching], for

reproof, for correction, for instruction in righteousness, that the man [or woman] of God
may be complete, thoroughly equipped for every good work. (2 Timothy 3:16–17)

But the Helper, the Holy Spirit, whom the Father will send in My [Jesus'] name, He will
teach you all things, and bring to your remembrance all things that I said to you. (John 14:26)

And you, fathers, do not provoke your children
to wrath, but bring them up in the training and
admonition of the Lord. (Ephesians 6:4)

LET'S ASK HIM:

Heavenly Papa, thank You for all Your very
special express delivery Father–love to us, Your
children. And special thanks for Your wonderful Father–love delivered to me, personally.

Again, I ask You to give me, by Your Spirit,
the unshakable faith to believe and trustingly
hang on to all that You have spoken and written
about Your unchangeable Father–Heart to me.
Enlarge, deepen, and protect my faith in You.

Daddy, give me an ever–growing passion to
love You in return, and an extravagant never–
dying thankfulness for Your great Father–love.

I ask this in all the wonderful victory, power,
and authority of Jesus' name.

CHAPTER SEVENTEEN

HEY GOD, DON'T YOU LOVE ME ANYMORE?

What About God's Chastening?

W
e ended the previous chapter with God's "Perfect Father Instruction." Now we will take a careful look at God's "Perfect Father Correction," which is a further part of Papa–God's perfect Father instruction.

It is very important that we rightly understand this expression of Papa–God's great eternal love for us, because satan works overtime on this subject, trying to get us to misunderstand or misinterpret God's corrections, and therefore reject God's loving, beneficial dealings with us. Satan, the deceiver, will try to convince us that God is punishing us and getting revenge, or that God doesn't love us anymore and we should just give up on Him.

GOD'S PERFECT FATHER CORRECTION

First let's look at the meaning of the words used in Scripture for this word, "correction." Various English translations render it as discipline, training, reproof, or chastening.

The Hebrew words for "correction" mean to make right, make pure, instruct, teach, convict of wrong, rebuke, reform, discipline, chasten (which means to purify, refine).

The Greek words for "correction" mean teach, educate, tutor, nurture, instruct, train, discipline, chasten (purify, refine).

IT IS NOT PUNISHMENT—
AND HE STILL LOVES YOU

Some English dictionaries make a clear distinction between "punishment" and "chastening," saying that to *punish* is to make one pay for his wrongdoings; but to *chasten* is wholly corrective and merciful in intent and result. This is a very important difference in meaning. Papa–God will lovingly chasten us for our greatest good and our highest benefit, but He will not make us pay for (punish us for) our failures and sins, because Jesus has already taken all the punishment and has fully paid for all our sins and failures when He died for us on the cross. Everyone who has received Jesus and His atoning death has been totally forgiven and washed white as snow.

> "Come now, and let us reason together," says the LORD, "Though your sins are like scarlet, they shall be as white as snow; though they are red like crimson, they shall be as wool." (Isaiah 1:18)

> Purge me with hyssop, and I shall be clean; wash me, and I shall be whiter than snow. (Psalm 51:7)

> The LORD is merciful and gracious, slow to anger, and abounding in mercy. He will not always strive with us, nor will He keep His anger forever. He has not dealt with us according to our sins, nor punished us according to our iniquities. For as the heavens are high above the

earth, so great is His mercy toward those who
fear [revere] Him; as far as the east is from the
west, so far has He removed our transgressions
from us. (Psalm 103:8–12)

It would be unjust for God to punish us after we have accepted Jesus' complete punishment for all our sins. But each of us needs His loving chastening (correction) for us to become all that He destined us to be—like Jesus.

Notice that chastening is far more constructive (teaching, training, encouraging, maturing, purifying) than it is corrective (reproof, rebuke, corporal discipline). It is corrective only when it needs to be. But remember that even then, it is always loving, merciful, and beneficial in its intent. Papa–God has promised to work all these things (what we do, what others do to us, or even what satan does to us) together for good—to transform us into the image of Jesus.

And we know that all things work together for
good to those who love God, to those who are
the called according to His purpose. For whom
He foreknew, He also predestined to be con-
formed to the image of His Son, that He might
be the firstborn among many brethren. (Romans 8:28–29)

I am emphasizing this because for many years as a Christian I greatly misunderstood and misinterpreted many of the things God was doing, or allowing for good, in my life. I mistakenly concluded that God was quite cranky, cruel, and vengeful. I have since found that many, many other Christians have also been deceived by the enemy in this same way. It is so important that we rightly understand Papa–God's loving correction (chastening) and receive it submissively and gratefully.

SO THEN, WHAT IS GOD'S CHASTENING?

Now let's look at what God Himself says in His Word about His correction and chastening:

> Behold, happy [blessed] is the man [or woman] whom God corrects; therefore do not despise the chastening of the Almighty. For He bruises, but He binds up; He wounds, but His hands make whole [well]. (Job 5:17–18)

It Is a Beneficial Blessing

Papa–God's correction is a blessing. It often does not feel nice or pleasant, but it is always beneficial, a gift of God's favor. Notice that the above Scripture says that God sometimes "bruises" and "wounds," but then God says that He does this in order to "make whole [well]." It is a blessing from Him—for our wholeness.

It Is for Our Healing and Well–Being

This is like a particular group of people in our society who are always cutting up other people's bodies, causing bleeding, bruising, and much acute pain. Quite often they cut out a part of a person's body and throw it away. Doesn't that sound horrible and sadistic? The people who do these things are called "surgeons." They are not cruel or mean. They do this only to heal, to give wholeness and health, and to save lives. How much greater is the goodness and loving compassion of our heavenly Surgeon–Father when He operates on us for our eternal health? Do not despise His chastening, because it is a blessing (in disguise).

It Is Another Express Delivery of His Love

Here is another Scripture about Papa–God's chastening:

> My son, do not despise the chastening of the LORD, nor detest His correction; for whom the LORD loves He corrects, just as a father [corrects] the son in whom he delights. (Proverbs 3:11–12)

Here, Papa–God tells us, His sons and daughters, not to despise or detest His chastening. He gives us a good reason why we shouldn't do so: it is because He loves us, His precious children. And because He loves us so much, He wants us to grow, develop, mature, and be spiritually healthy, well, and whole, and to become all that He has destined us to be. Let's face it, we all need lots of teaching, training, developing, correcting, and (from time to time) some "spiritual surgery"—for our own good and for God's glory.

This Scripture also says that our great loving Papa–God corrects us because He delights in us, His dear children. "Delight" means intense joy and pleasure. Our Papa–God delights in our spiritual maturing, healing, and wholeness, just like the delight the surgeon must feel when he sees a person whose life his surgery has saved and who had been made well and strong again.

It Is for Our Greatest Good and Highest Benefit

Here is the most complete Scripture on Papa–God's chastening:

> And you have forgotten the exhortation which speaks to you as to sons [children]: "My son [or daughter], do not despise the chastening of the LORD, nor be discouraged when you are rebuked by Him; for whom the LORD loves He chastens, and scourges [disciplines] every son whom He receives." If you endure chastening, God deals with you as with sons; for what son is there whom a father does not chasten? But if you are without chastening, of which all have become partakers, then you are illegitimate and not [true] sons. Furthermore, we have had human fathers who corrected us, and we paid them respect. Shall we not much more readily be in subjection to the Father of [our] spirits and live? For they indeed for a few days chastened us as seemed best to them, but He for our profit, that we may be partakers of His holiness [wholeness]. Now no chastening seems to be joyful for the present, but painful; nevertheless, afterward it yields the peaceable fruit of righteousness to those who have been trained by it. Therefore strengthen the hands which hang down, and the feeble knees, and make straight paths for your feet, so that what is lame may not be dislocated, but rather be healed. (Hebrews 12:5–13)

He disciplines us because He loves us so much. He is not rejecting us. He is receiving us, imperfect as we are, and lovingly working in us to purify us and transform us into the likeness of Jesus.

It Is Far Better than That of
Any Good Earthly Father

Papa–God uses the correction of a good, loving human father as an illustration of His far higher and more perfect correction of us, His children. He makes it very clear that *all* of His true children will receive His loving, beneficial instruction and correction. Here is another Scripture to encourage us:

> No temptation [testing, trial] has overtaken you except such as is common to man; but God is faithful, who will not allow you to be tempted beyond what you are able, but with the temptation [testing, trial] will also make the way of escape, that you may be able to bear it. (1 Corinthians 10:13)

It Is Always Very Compassionate and Tender

Papa–God also lets us know in Hebrews 12:11 that He fully understands that chastening (discipline) is not "joyful" (pleasant) at the time, but rather "painful" (and grievous). This is the time to stubbornly remember that our loving Papa–God is compassionate, tender, and understanding, and that He is not being hard, uncaring, and unfeeling. He feels for us and with us. He will be as gentle as possible, but as tough as He needs to be to get the job done. One of the smartest things we can ever do is repent quickly. This can save us a lot of unpleasant chastening.

It Is Always for Our Highest Eternal Benefit

It is extremely important that we believe and remember that our infinitely loving heavenly Father is chastening us for our profit (our benefit and betterment) and for our eternal good. He has great, high, and eternal purposes in mind for us, which are unimaginably worth all these temporary unpleasant and grievous times of training and correction. In Hebrews 12:10–13, our loving Papa–God also says that He does all this *"that we may be partakers of His holiness [wholeness],"* that He may produce in us *"the peaceable fruit of righteousness,"* and *"so that what is lame may not be dislocated [broken], but rather be healed [made whole]."* Our great, good Father does these things to us because He loves us too much to leave us in the same condition as when we repented and He lovingly received us. He has far greater, better, and higher purposes and destinies for us than we can imagine. Here is another encouraging Scripture:

> Therefore we do not lose heart. Even though our outward man is perishing, yet the inward man [person] is being renewed day by day. For our light affliction, which is but for a moment, is working for us a far more exceeding and eternal weight of glory, while we do not look at the things which are seen, but at the things which are not seen. For the things which are seen are temporary, but the things

which are not seen are eternal. (2 Corinthians 4:16–18)

It Is for All of Us, Without Exception

Our perfect Papa–God will surely, faithfully, lovingly, and beneficially teach us, train us, develop us, purify us, mature us, and correct us. It is not optional. He said that this is for *every* child *"whom He receives"* (Hebrews 12:7–8). Jesus said, *"As many as I love, I rebuke and chasten"* (Revelation 3:19).

WHAT SHOULD BE OUR RESPONSE?

The extent of the benefits from God's training and correction will depend on how we respond to His training and correction. We choose these responses with our free will. In Hebrews 12:1–13 and Revelation 3:19, Papa–God exhorts (earnestly urges) us as to how we should respond:

- …lay aside every weight, and the sin which so easily ensnares us.

- …run with endurance [patience] the race that is set before us.

- …[look] unto Jesus, the author and finisher [perfecter] of our faith.

- …consider Him [Jesus] who endured… lest you become weary and discouraged.

- …do not despise the chastening of the LORD.

- …[do not] be discouraged when you are rebuked by Him.

- …endure [go through it all the way] [God's] chastening.

- …be in subjection [submission] to the Father.

- …strengthen the hands which hang down, and the feeble knees [don't give in to weariness and discouragement].

- …make straight paths for your feet [so you won't stumble].

- …be zealous and repent.

GOD'S CHASTENING—ILLUSTRATED

Keep in mind these Scriptural illustrations:

- An athlete being trained by a coach, to succeed and win (1 Corinthians 9:24–27).

- A soldier being trained by a sergeant, to survive and conquer (2 Timothy 2:3–4).

- An employee being trained to profit and please his employer (2 Timothy 2:15).

- Children being trained and matured by their parents, to become all that they were destined to be (Ephesians 6:4).

The coach, the sergeant, the employer, and the parents are not being mean and nasty by insisting on the instruction, training, conditioning, testings, correcting, and discipline. It is only so that their protégés will survive, develop, and succeed. So it is with our Papa–God and His perfect ways of dealing with us. He does this because He loves us so greatly and has great destinies for us all.

God's loving chastening and training may involve any or all of the following aspects: teaching, training, conditioning, testing, demonstration, rebuke, and, if necessary, spanking.

Teaching: Developing Knowledge

Papa–God teaches us through:

- His written Word (2 Timothy 2:15, 3:16–17)

- His Holy Spirit within us (John 14:26)

- His appointed teachers (Ephesians 4:11–16)

- Our fellow disciples (Matthew 28:19–20)

- The circumstances and experiences of life—*both* our failures and our successes

Our Papa–God lovingly and patiently teaches and instructs us to prepare us for spiritual growth, maturity, and success.

Training: Developing Skills

Papa–God not only imparts knowledge to us, but He also gets us to do and practice what we learn and be *"doers of the word, and not hearers only"* (James 1:22). Along with "classroom" teaching, He, in many various ways, gives us practical assignments to develop our skills. Our Papa–God lovingly prepares us for spiritual effectiveness and fruitfulness.

Conditioning: Developing Endurance

Sometimes Papa–God will leave us in a difficult situation for a period of time or allow troubles to come to us again and again, in order to develop patience, stamina, tenacity, and endurance (Romans 5:3–4). It is much like a coach making athletes run around the track again and again, day after day, until they almost drop. It is also like a sergeant making his soldiers go on long, hard marches with heavy packs to develop endurance and strength. Our Papa–God lovingly prepares us for spiritual strength and survival.

Testing: Developing Confidence

Many times, God allows situations to test us. The Greek word translated as "temptation" also means trial or test. These trials are not for God to know how we are doing (He already knows all our thoughts, intents, weaknesses, and actions), but for us to know and to demonstrate to us how we are developing and in what areas we are still weak. It is like a schoolteacher giving an exam, and then showing the students how well or how poorly they are learning, and also what to do about their deficiencies (1 Peter 1:6–7, 4:12–13). These tests, and even our failures, can be great lessons which further develop us. Our Papa–God *always* lovingly develops our character and maturity for our highest good.

Demonstration: Developing Examples to Others

Sometimes Papa–God will put us through a difficult situation not only to prove to us how He is developing us, but also to demonstrate to those around us the beautiful difference that Jesus has made, and is making, in our lives. This is a living demonstration to the truth of our verbal witnessing about Jesus. Our Papa–God always lovingly uses us to be His living witnesses—by words *and* deeds.

> Let your light so shine before men, that they may see your good works and glorify your Father in heaven. (Matthew 5:16)

Rebuke: A Verbal Correction

When we are sinning, failing, or doing something wrong, Papa–God will lovingly rebuke us or give us some kind of verbal reproof to correct us. This can come in different ways: God pricking our conscience, the Holy Spirit convicting us within, or God speaking to us through a Scripture, a sermon, a fellow believer, a book, a song, or in some other way.

Here is an important word of caution: the devil is called *"the accuser of [the] brethren [believers]"* (Revelation 12:10), and he will try to counterfeit the conviction of the Holy Spirit. He will be accusing and condemning us to produce discouragement and hopelessness—aimed at getting us to give up on God. The true conviction of the Holy Spirit will always be urging us to repent (turn back to God), confess, and ask the Father to forgive and cleanse us (1 John 1:9), whereas the devil will try to put us down and keep us down. Refuse him! The Spirit of

God will always lift us up and restore us (John 16:8, 12–14). Allow Him to correct you and restore you. Our Papa–God lovingly reproves us to develop our wholeness (holiness). He still loves us greatly, even though sometimes it doesn't feel like it.

Spanking: A Corporal Correction

Our loving Papa–God is very patient and longsuffering, but if we continue to ignore or rebel against the convictions of His Holy Spirit (His verbal corrections), He will have to eventually use some kind of corporal discipline to bring us to repentance. Hebrews 12 says that *"whom the LORD [Father] loves He chastens, and scourges [spanks] every son [child] whom He receives"* (Hebrews 12:6).

Even in these more extreme measures of correction, Papa–God is still loving us and doing us good. Always remember that Papa–God's corrective chastening, without exception, is His love in action. It is always for our greatest eternal good and for His highest purposes. He is not rejecting you nor punishing you, but purifying and developing you and "growing you up." Never consider God's chastening as anything but His love and for your good. He has promised to *"work [all things] together for good to those who love God, to those who are the called according to His purpose"* (Romans 8:28). Submit to Him. Trust Him. Look for good to come out of it. He will be faithful. He still truly loves you. He will never quit loving you—no, never. It is His very nature! He will not break His New Covenant with us (Psalm 89:30–34)!

God's Dealings May Be for Reasons Beyond Our Understanding

Sometimes God, in His infinite wisdom, may put us through, or allow us to go through, situations that are not His instruction or His correction, but may be for some other purpose of His that is beyond our current understanding. He uses us in various ways to demonstrate and witness Jesus to the dark, unbelieving world around us, and to fight, defeat, and "plunder" the kingdom of satan (Mark 3:27). No matter what happens, continue to submit to your great, loving Papa–God. Trust Him. Don't give up. He still loves you.

Jesus is our greatest example. Even though He was sinless, *"yet He learned obedience by the things which He suffered"* (Hebrews 5:8).

> For to this you were called, because Christ also suffered for us, leaving us an example, that you should follow His steps. (1 Peter 2:21)

LET'S ASK HIM:

> Heavenly Father, my great, totally–loving Papa, help me to really understand and to always remember that Your instruction, training, correction, and chastening is always Your great, true love at work for my greatest good and my highest eternal benefit.

> Enable me, by the power of Your Spirit, to trustingly submit to You and to what You are doing in me.

Also, empower me to not despise Your chastening, nor be discouraged, nor let satan get me down and keep me down. Jesus, keep lifting me up and bringing me back to my loving, patient, forgiving Papa.

Help me to trust Your love, Your wisdom, and Your guidance in the process of Your training, developing, and maturing me into all that You want me to be.

Daddy, give me all the encouragement, strength, faith, and endurance I will need. I thank You that You will always be faithful to do this.

I ask this in the name of my wonderful, victorious, loving Savior, Jesus Christ.

CHAPTER EIGHTEEN

LIKE FATHER, LIKE SON

The Ultimate Expression of God's Father-Heart

GOD THE FATHER REVEALED HIMSELF TO US IN HUMAN FLESH

Before the beginning ever began, *"the Word was with God, and the Word was God... And the Word became flesh... full of grace and truth"* (John 1:1, 14). And the Word was Jesus.

In the beginning was the Word, and the Word was with God, and the Word was God. He was in the beginning with God. All things were made through Him, and without Him nothing was made that was made. In Him was life, and the life was the light of men. (John 1:1–4)

And the Word [Jesus] became flesh and dwelt among us, and we beheld His glory, the glory as of the only begotten of the Father, full of grace and truth. (John 1:14)

He [Jesus] was clothed with a robe dipped in blood, and His name is called The Word of God. (Revelation 19:13)

God named Him "Jesus," which means "God saves." And God also called Jesus "Immanuel," which means "God with us" (Matthew 1:21–23).

The great eternal Creator manifested, revealed, and expressed Himself to us, His earthly children, in such a marvelous way so that we could see and understand His wonderful Father-Heart. He came right down onto our level—as a human. This is a great mystery that surpasses human comprehension. It is God's great, Father-Love—in action.

> And without controversy great is the mystery of godliness: God was manifested in the flesh, justified in [authenticated by] the Spirit, seen by angels [the messengers], preached among the Gentiles, believed on in the world, received up in glory. (1 Timothy 3:16)

JESUS "IS COME IN THE FLESH"

This great and amazing truth is absolutely foundational and essential. See what God says about it:

> Beloved, do not believe every spirit, but test the spirits, whether they are of God; because many false prophets have gone out into the world. By this you know the Spirit of God: Every spirit that confesses [proclaims] that Jesus Christ has [is] come in the flesh is of God, and every spirit that does not confess [proclaim] that Jesus Christ has [is] come in the flesh is not of God. And this is the spirit of the Antichrist, which

you have heard was coming, and is now already
in the world. (1 John 4:1–3)

Notice that in the above Scripture, God says that those
who do not confess (do not acknowledge) that Jesus Christ is
come in the flesh are "not of God." God does not say those who
deny it, but those who just do not proclaim it. (If any person,
prophet, or minister leaves out this essential identity of Jesus
Christ in their ministry, we would be wise not to trust them.)

The verb tense of "has come in the flesh" is not rendered
in simple past tense, but is a past–present tense, meaning that
Jesus has come in the flesh and is still in the flesh. (The King
James Version of the Bible translates it as "*is* come in the flesh.")

JESUS SAID, "I AND MY FATHER ARE ONE"

These are the proclamations of Jesus Himself:

I and my Father are one. (John 10:30)

Most assuredly, I say to you, the Son can do
nothing of Himself, but what He sees the Father do; for whatever He does, the Son also
does in like manner. For the Father loves the
Son, and shows Him all things that He Himself
does... (John 5:19–20)

For I have come down from heaven, not to do
My own will, but the will of Him who sent Me.
(John 6:38)

Jesus answered them and said, "My doctrine [teaching] is not Mine, but His who sent Me." (John 7:16)

If you had known Me, you would have known My Father also. (John 8:19)

Then Jesus said to them, "When you lift up [crucify] the Son of Man, then you will know that I am He, and that I do nothing of Myself; but as My Father taught Me, I speak these things." (John 8:28)

And he who sees Me sees Him who sent Me. (John 12:45)

For I have not spoken on My own authority; but the Father who sent Me gave Me a command, what I should say and what I should speak. (John 12:49)

…he who receives Me receives Him who sent Me. (John 13:20)

He who has seen Me has seen the Father; so how can you say, "Show us the Father"? Do you not believe that I am in the Father, and the Father in Me? (John 14:9–10)

For the Father judges no one, but has committed all judgment to the Son, that all should honor the Son just as they honor the Father. He who does not honor the Son does not honor the Father who sent Him. (John 5:22–23)

The above Scriptures are just a few of many similar ones in the Gospel of John. Jesus made it very clear and unmistakable about Who He is: *He is God the Father, manifest in the flesh.*

OUR FATHER'S GREATEST GIFT— NEVER STOPS GIVING

God, our Father, so loved the world that He gave, and *gave*, and is still **giving** us His Only Begotten Son.

> For God so loved the world that He gave His only begotten Son [Jesus], that whoever believes in Him should not perish but have everlasting life. For God did not send His Son into the world to condemn the world, but that the world through Him might be saved. (John 3:16–17)

> [Christ Jesus], being in the form of God, did not consider it robbery to be equal with God, but made Himself of no reputation, taking the form of a bondservant [slave], and coming in the likeness of men. And being found in appearance as a man, He humbled Himself and became obedient to the point of death, even the death of the cross. Therefore God also has highly exalted Him and given Him the name which is above every name, that at the name of Jesus every knee should bow, of those in heav-

en, and of those on earth, and of those under the earth, and that every tongue should confess that Jesus Christ is Lord, to the glory of God the Father. (Philippians 2:6–11)

God Gave Us His Son to Be Born as a Human

Our Father *gave* His Son, Jesus, to us through the virgin Mary (conceived by the Holy Spirit), to be born a flesh–and–blood human, in a Bethlehem cattle shed, and laid in a manger, a cattle feeding trough (Matthew 1:18–25; Luke 2:4–7).

God Gave Us His Son to Live Among Us in His Fullness

Then our Father *gave* His Son, Jesus, to us to live among us and to teach, heal, and deliver, in order to fully manifest His Father's Heart to us—in the flesh. Jesus was not a vision or an apparition, or even an angel. He had a real human body, soul, and spirit. He was a real man, right down on our level—not as a superman, but as a sinless man through whom God could fully demonstrate His great, true love to us.

For in Him [Jesus] dwells all the fullness of the Godhead [divine nature] bodily. (Colossians 2:9)

God Gave Us His Son to Be Crucified for Our Sins

Then the Father *gave* His Son, Jesus, to us as the full atonement for our sins—crucified in the flesh and buried in a tomb for three days and three nights while His soul paid for our sins in the depths of hell. He took on Himself all our sin, our guilt, and our spiritual death (Isaiah 53:4–11; 1 Peter 3:18).

God Gave Us His Son to Be Raised from the Dead, Triumphant

Then the Father *gave* His Son, Jesus, to us, raised physically from the dead as a victorious, living Savior in a resurrected, incorruptible body. After His resurrection, Jesus said to His disciples, *"Behold My hands and My feet, that it is I Myself. Handle Me and see, for a spirit does not have flesh and bones as you see I have"* (Luke 24:39).

> …to [the apostles] He also presented Himself alive after His suffering by many infallible proofs, being seen by them during forty days and speaking of the things pertaining to the kingdom of God. (Acts 1:3)

God Gives Us His Son to Be Lord of All

Now the Father *gives* His Son, Jesus, to us, ascended in His glorified resurrection body as the supreme, reigning, triumphant King, far above every other name.

> He [God] raised Him [Jesus] from the dead and seated Him at His right hand in the heavenly places, far above all principality and power and might and dominion, and every name that is named, not only in this age but also in that which is to come. And He put all things under His feet, and gave Him to be head over

all things to the church. (Ephesians 1:20–22)

The LORD said to my Lord [Jesus], "Sit at My right hand, till I make Your enemies Your footstool"... (Matthew 22:44)

For He must reign till He has put all enemies under His feet. (1 Corinthians 15:25)

God Gives Us His Son to Be Our Compassionate Intercessor

God *gives* Jesus to us as our elder brother in the flesh, representing us humans to His Father and interceding for us as our great High Priest. Jesus, the eternal Son of God, is right now seated with the Father in His resurrected, glorified human body, interceding and reigning until He returns bodily to reign on earth as King of kings and Lord of lords.

Inasmuch then as the children have partaken of flesh and blood, He Himself likewise shared in the same... Therefore, in all things He had to be made like His brethren [us], that He might be a merciful and faithful High Priest in things pertaining to God... (Hebrews 2:14, 17)

But He, because He continues forever, has an unchangeable priesthood. Therefore He is also able to save to the uttermost [completely] those who come to God through Him, since He always lives to make intercession for them. (Hebrews 7:24–25)

Who is he who condemns? It is Christ who died, and furthermore is also risen, who is even at the right hand of God, who also makes intercession for us. (Romans 8:34)

God Will Give Us His Son to Return and Be Ruler of the Whole Earth

And God *will give* Jesus to us when He returns to earth in His glorified body to reign over the whole world in righteousness for a thousand years as King of kings and Lord of lords.

Now when He [Jesus] had spoken these things, while they [the apostles] watched, He was taken up, and a cloud received Him out of their sight. And while they looked steadfastly toward heaven as He went up, behold, two men stood by them in white apparel, who also said, "Men of Galilee, why do you stand gazing up into heaven? This same Jesus, who was taken up from you into heaven, will so come in like manner as you saw Him go into heaven." (Acts 1:9–11)

Behold, He is coming with clouds, and every eye will see Him. (Revelation 1:7)

And He has on His robe and on His thigh a name written: KING OF KINGS AND LORD OF LORDS. (Revelation 19:16)

Blessed and holy is he who has part in the first resurrection. Over such the second death has no power, but they shall be priests of God and of Christ, and shall reign with Him a thousand years. (Revelation 20:6)

So Jesus *has* come in the flesh, *was* crucified in the flesh, *was* resurrected in the flesh, *is* now reigning in heaven in His glorified body, and *will* come back to rule over the whole earth in His glorified body.

THE FULL EXPRESSION AND DEMONSTRATION (THE WORD) OF THE FATHER

Jesus Is the Visible Image of the Invisible God, Our Creator

He [Jesus] is the image of the invisible God, the firstborn over all creation. For by Him all things were created that are in heaven and that are on earth, visible and invisible, whether thrones or dominions or principalities or powers. All things were created through Him and for Him. And He is before all things, and in Him all things consist. And He is the head of the body, the church, who is the beginning, the firstborn from the dead, that in all things He may have the preeminence. For it pleased the Father that in Him all the fullness should dwell. (Colossians 1:15–19)

Jesus Is the Brightness of God's Glory and the Exact Image of the Father's Heart

[Jesus] being the brightness of His [the Father's] glory and the express image of His person. (Hebrews 1:3)

Jesus Is the Glory of the Father, Full of Grace and Truth

And the Word [Jesus] became flesh and dwelt among us, and we beheld His glory, the glory as of the only begotten of the Father, full of grace and truth. (John 1:14)

Jesus Is All the Fullness of the Father in Bodily Form

For in Him [Jesus] dwells all the fullness of the Godhead [divine nature] bodily; and you are complete in Him, who is the head of all principality and power. (Colossians 2:9–10)

The Father Was in Jesus, Reconciling Us unto Himself

…God was in Christ reconciling the world to Himself, not imputing [attributing, crediting] their trespasses to them, and has committed to us the word of reconciliation. (2 Corinthians 5:19)

Do you not believe that I [Jesus] am in the Father, and the Father in Me? (John 14:10)

The Father Gave His Holy Spirit to Jesus in Full Measure

For He [Jesus] whom God has sent speaks the words of God, for God does not give [Him] the Spirit by [limited] measure. (John 3:34)

Jesus Was Always in Intimate Union with the Father

Jesus consistently, in talking to and teaching the people, referred to God as "Father," which was very radical and offensive to the Jewish religious leaders of His day. In every prayer of Jesus recorded in all four Gospels, Jesus addressed God as "Father." And praying in the garden of Gethsemane, He even called God "Abba," which was the Aramaic word children commonly used to lovingly address their fathers. The equivalent of this word in English today would be "Papa" or "Daddy."

And He [Jesus] said, "Abba, Father, all things are possible for You. Take this cup away from Me; nevertheless, not what I will, but what You will." (Mark 14:36)

The Father Encourages Us Also to Call Him "Papa"

God has given to us this same expression of intimate endearment—"Abba," "Papa"—by His Holy Spirit, whom He has put in our hearts.

But when the fullness of the time had come, God sent forth His Son, born of a woman, born under the law, to redeem those who were under the law, that we might receive the adoption as sons. And because you are sons, God has sent forth the Spirit of His Son into your hearts, crying out, "Abba, Father!" (Galatians 4:4–6)

For you did not receive the spirit of bondage again to fear, but you received the Spirit of adoption by whom we cry out, "Abba, Father." The Spirit Himself bears witness with our spirit that we are children of God. (Romans 8:15–16)

JESUS IS OUR PERFECT PATTERN TO RELATE TO OUR ABBA FATHER

Jesus' close, loving, submissive relationship with His Abba is our great example to follow. Jesus said:

"As the Father has sent Me, I also send you." And when He had said this, He breathed on them [the disciples], and said to them, "Receive the Holy Spirit." (John 20:21–22)

…I honor My Father… And I do not seek My own glory. (John 8:49–50)

Most assuredly, I say to you, the Son can do nothing of Himself, but what He sees the Father do; for whatever He does, the Son also does in like manner… I can of Myself do nothing. As I hear, I judge; and My judgment is righteous, because I do not seek My own will but the will of the Father who sent Me. (John 5:19, 30)

...I always do those things that please Him. (John 8:29)

Therefore, whatever I speak, just as the Father has told Me, so I speak. (John 12:50)

For I have come down from heaven, not to do My own will, but the will of Him who sent me. (John 6:38)

Sacrifice and offering You did not desire, but a body You have prepared for Me... Then I said, "Behold, I have come... to do your will, O God." (Hebrews 10:5, 7)

A GREAT DIVINE MYSTERY

Let's not try to figure this all out with our very limited human logic and reasoning. This wonderful truth is too high and deep for our human comprehension. Simply believe it and experience it, because God spoke it, wrote it, and preserved it in His Scriptures for us today.

And without controversy great is the mystery of godliness: God was manifested in the flesh, justified in [authenticated by] the Spirit, seen by angels [the messengers], preached among the Gentiles, believed on in the world, received up in glory. (1 Timothy 3:16)

THE ONLY WAY BACK TO THE FATHER

Now let's take a look at a very important statement that Jesus made:

> I am the way [to the Father], the truth [about the Father], and the life [of the Father]. No one comes to the Father except through Me. (John 14:6)

The whole context of the above Scripture verse is John 14:1–11, which speaks of the Father's house, seeing the Father, and the way to the Father. So the insertions in brackets that I have added to the above Scripture are based on the context and give a clearer understanding of what Jesus is really saying.

By His crucifixion for our sins, His burial, and His resurrection, Jesus made the only way for us to come to the Father and be forgiven, received, and joyfully welcomed by Him.

> For Christ also suffered once for sins, the just for the unjust, that He might bring us to God, being put to death in the flesh but made alive by the Spirit. (1 Peter 3:18)

> For there is one God and one Mediator between God and men, the Man Christ Jesus, who gave Himself a ransom for all, to be testified in due time. (1 Timothy 2:5–6)

> Nor is there salvation in any other, for there is no other name under heaven given among men by which we must be saved. (Acts 4:12)

THE ULTIMATE REVELATION OF THE
WONDERFUL FATHER-HEART OF GOD

Look carefully at Jesus and see the inexpressibly wonderful, true, faithful, loving, tender Heart of our Father. I urge you to read through the four Gospels—Matthew, Mark, Luke, and John—looking at and listening to Jesus and seeing the fullness of the Father expressed and demonstrated through Him in word and in deed. Even the Old Testament Scriptures have much to say about Jesus: The One who was yet to come, the Messiah, the Sent One from the Father. The rest of the New Testament also gives us much more insight into who Jesus is and what He did for us by His crucifixion, resurrection, and ascension.

Look at Jesus' way of life—His actions, His attitudes, His deeds, His way of relating to various kinds of people—and *see* the loving Papa–God in action.

Look at Jesus' character, His nature, His disposition, and His attitudes, and *see* the Father's beautiful nature and surpassing goodness—His true love.

Listen to Jesus' teaching and preaching—even His denunciation of the proud, harsh, legalistic religionists—and hear the Father's thoughts, feelings, values, and priorities toward His children on the one hand, and those religionists on the other.

Ponder the ministries of Jesus, His love and compassion, His friendship with sinners, His preaching the Gospel to the poor, His healing of the sick, His deliverance of those tormented by satan, His comforting of those who mourned, His hugging and blessing the little children—and *see* the very core of our Father's great Heart of compassion, tender mercy, abounding grace, free forgiveness, overflowing goodness, and eternal kindness.

And then, *carefully consider* Jesus' awful crucifixion, His terrible suffering, His bearing *"our sins in His own body on the tree [cross]"* (1 Peter 2:24), *"the just for the unjust"* (1 Peter 3:18), His blood being shed as the atonement for the sins of *"the whole world"* (1 John 2:2), and His sinless soul being made the complete offering for our sins (Isaiah 53:10). *See* God laying on Jesus *"the iniquity of us all"* (Isaiah 53:6) and begin to realize and comprehend *"the width and length and depth and height—to know the love of Christ which passes knowledge"* (Ephesians 3:18–19). Read Chapter 14 again.

See how Jesus took all our sin, condemnation, guilt, and judgment; how He took our place, our death, and our hell; how He purchased for us, with His precious shed blood, our complete forgiveness, our eternal salvation, our spiritual birth into the Father's family, and our total acceptance into the great, eager, welcoming, loving arms of our Heavenly Papa.

Begin to fathom how unimaginably great was the price our Father paid to win us back into the arms of His intense, passionate love, how extremely precious each one of us must be to our Papa, and of what extremely high value and great worth we are, for Him to do all this to His beloved Son—for us. How greatly our Papa rejoices and delights in us when we return to Him and receive Jesus and His great eternal love.

Jesus is the ultimate demonstration of our Father's infinite Heart of love for us and His incredibly intense yearning, burning desire, and deep longing for us to be reconciled back into His arms of eternal love again.

Now *see* Jesus victorious, triumphant, and resurrected

from death and hell. *See* His glorious ascension back to the throne of God in heaven, receiving from the Father all power, authority, dominion, and the name which is far above every name, and begin to know:

> ...what is the exceeding greatness of His [the Father's] power toward us who believe, according to the working of His mighty power which He worked in Christ when He raised Him from the dead and seated Him at His right hand in the heavenly places, far above all principality and power and might and dominion, and every name that is named, not only in this age but also in that which is to come. And He put all things under His feet, and gave Him to be head over all things to the church, which is His body, the fullness of Him who fills all in all. (Ephesians 1:19–23)

Our Heavenly Papa is fully and completely as true, loving, forgiving, merciful, gracious, tender, kind, compassionate, beautiful, and good as Jesus is. They are one and the same. Jesus is the Father manifesting Himself to us in flesh and blood.

How Can We Receive the Father and Be Received By Him?

Turn Your Heart Back to God Your Father

Turn your heart wholeheartedly back to God your Father and be willing to go God's way instead of your own. This is what the Bible calls repentance. It is what we call a U-turn. The will to repent, and the power to repent, are gifts from God to those who want to repent. Ask Him for genuine repentance. Commit yourself to follow Jesus and become His disciple (follower).

> …[God] now commands all men everywhere to repent, because He has appointed a day on which He will judge the world in righteousness by the Man [Jesus] whom He has ordained. He has given assurance of this to all by raising Him from the dead. (Acts 17:30–31)

> The Lord is not slack concerning His promise, as some count slackness, but is longsuffering toward us, not willing that any should perish but that all should come to repentance. (2 Peter 3:9)

> …repent, turn to God, and do works befitting repentance. (Acts 26:20)

Believe in Jesus

Believe in Jesus, in His crucifixion for the forgiveness of your sins, and in His resurrection for your salvation. This is more than just accepting that God exists and that Jesus lived and died. Scripture says that even the demons believe that God exists—and tremble (James 2:19).

"Believe in," in the Scriptural sense, means put faith in, trust in, depend upon, rely upon. This type of belief—faith—is not something you can do on your own. He gives faith to those who want to believe. It is a decision you choose to make with God's help. Depend on Jesus' crucifixion for your salvation.

For Christ also suffered once for sins, the just for the unjust, that He might bring us to God, being put to death in the flesh but made alive by the Spirit. (1 Peter 3:18)

In Him [Jesus] we have redemption through His blood, the forgiveness of sins, according to the riches of His grace. (Ephesians 1:7)

But what does it [faith] say? "The word is near you, in your mouth and in your heart" (that is, the word of faith which we preach): that if you confess with your mouth the Lord Jesus and believe in your heart that God has raised Him from the dead, you will be saved. For with the heart one believes unto righteousness, and with the mouth confession is made unto salvation. (Romans 10:8–10)

For God so loved the world that He gave His only begotten Son [Jesus], that whoever believes in Him should not perish but have everlasting life. For God did not send His Son into the world to condemn the world, but that the world through Him might be saved. (John 3:16–17)

For by grace you have been saved through faith, and that [faith] not of yourselves; it is the gift of God, not of works, lest anyone should boast. (Ephesians 2:8–9)

Receive Jesus by Faith

Receive Jesus by faith. Open wide your heart. Invite Him in. This is not just mentally accepting a statement of theology or joining a church; this is whole-heartedly receiving the living person of Jesus and beginning a personal relationship with Him and, through Him, with the Father. This personal relationship also means giving yourself to Jesus and the Father to follow and obey Them. Both of Them will eagerly, joyfully, and completely receive you, because the very moment you receive Jesus as the atonement (payment) for your sins, you are completely forgiven, cleansed, and justified (declared righteous). You are then spiritually born again by the Holy Spirit (John 3:3–8) into the Father's family.

> Most assuredly, I [Jesus] say to you… he who receives Me receives Him [the Father] who sent Me. (John 13:20)

> But as many as received Him [Jesus], to them He gave the right to become children of God, to those who believe in His name: who were born, not of blood, nor of the will of the flesh, nor of the will of man, but of God. (John 1:12–13)

> Behold, I [Jesus] stand at the door and knock. If anyone hears My voice and opens the door, I will come in to him and dine [feast] with him, and he with Me. (Revelation 3:20)

> If we confess our sins [express repentance], He is faithful and just to forgive us our sins and to

cleanse us from all unrighteousness. (1 John 1:9)

For the wages of sin is [eternal] death, but the gift of God is eternal life in Christ Jesus our Lord. (Romans 6:23)

LET'S ASK HIM:

Thank You, thank You, thank You, Father, for giving Yourself, for revealing Yourself, and for demonstrating Yourself to us through Jesus Christ.

Thank You for manifesting to us Your wonderful loving Father–Heart, through the life and death of Your beloved Son.

Cause me to increasingly see, believe, and receive Your indescribable, infinite, true, astounding love and goodness.

Spirit of God, enable me to wholeheartedly return to my Heavenly Papa and by faith receive His Son, Jesus—His crucifixion and His resurrection—as the full atonement for my sins.

Jesus, I wholeheartedly receive you into my heart and life as my Creator, my God, my Savior, and my Lord, and I give myself and my life back to You, to follow You as Your disciple.

Holy Spirit, come in and unite with my spirit to make me a new creation in Jesus. Change me as only You can and fill me to overflowing. Really drench me!

Daddy, give me increasingly more of Your loving Heart in my heart, more of Jesus' wonderful life in my life, and more of Your Holy Spirit's transforming power in my earthly weakness.

I ask this in Jesus' all-powerful name.

CHAPTER NINETEEN

GOD ILLUSTRATES BEING IN HIS ARMS

Two Visions of God's Astounding Love

INTRODUCTION

As I was finishing the last few chapters of this book, God graciously gave two wonderful visions to my dear son, Paul. Paul has had a long and terrible struggle throughout his life with self–rejection, despair, and depression. I have walked with him though much of this and have loved him, wept, prayed, and trusted God for his complete deliverance and inner healing. Through this journey, I myself have learned and experienced much of God's tender, loving Father–Heart for us, His children.

During these last few years, God has done a deep work in Paul and has given him a great measure of deliverance, healing, and the Holy Spirit. This is now evident by his consistent, loving, transformed life, and his loving ministry to others.

God confirmed His great work in Paul by showing him these two vivid visions, which are sharply contrasting but closely connected. The extreme before–and–after contrast of these two pictures is very powerful, and whenever shared they have had a profound effect on many people.

These two visions were given just as my manuscript was

being completed, so they didn't influence the book. And he had not yet read the manuscript, so the book didn't influence the visions.

But because these two visions fit so well with the theme of this book—namely, the wonderful salvation and deliverance of Jesus and the immeasurable goodness and love of God—he and I prayed, and God clearly guided us to add them to the end of this book, as a wonderful illustration of God's great, loving, true, and faithful Father–Heart.

I quote Paul: "Both of these pictures were so deeply personal that I had no intention of ever sharing them, even with those closest to me—but God had other plans."

THE FIRST VISION:

A Dark Picture of My Past: Drowning in Dreadful Darkness

by Paul Hutchinson

As this vision started, I had a great sense of darkness, dread, fear, anger, hopelessness, depression, and deep loneliness. The scene opens as though I am drifting downwards through a space which is total blackness in all directions. Soon there is enough grayness for me to see what is happening. There, to my shock, is myself! I am struggling violently to stay afloat in a vast, horrible, dark, slimy sea of sewage, serpents, vileness, and torments. I am straining to keep from drowning, thrashing about wildly and screaming, feeling my strength draining, and sensing that I am in a sea that is endless in all directions.

I am angry, in great pain (physically and mentally), screaming angrily at God, even cursing God, and blaming

Him for all my misery. I scream, "Why? Where are You? Why don't You care?" An endless stream of pain is coming from deep within me.

As I watch this scene, I am struck with two horrors. First, I am cursing God and saying such horrible things to Him and about Him. The second horror strikes me very much deeper, for I have, in my life, actually done and said these very things to Him! I am almost unable to continue watching, because the pain, remorse, regret, guilt, shame, and sorrow are overwhelming me.

As much as I don't want to, I keep on looking and see that I continue screaming and thrashing. As I try to look away from this scene of torture, there is enough light now to see more of the picture. And now I see Jesus. He is dressed all in pure white, standing either on this sea of vileness or on a solid rock. Jesus calls out my name, but in my thrashing and screaming I can't seem to hear Him. He continues to call my name and reach out to me, but in this dark, vile sea, I also seem unable to see Him.

I am horrified as I watch Jesus come so close to me that my thrashing and struggling are splashing this dark, stinking, vile muck onto Him, and I am still unaware that He is there. But Jesus looks at me with all the more love and gets even closer, reaching out to me even though more black muck is getting on Him.

As He begins to gently and lovingly pull me out of this sea of torture, my flailing hits Him, and even strikes Him across the face with slime and muck. But even now, He is still smiling lovingly at me, and I still don't realize He is there. I am still kicking and thrashing as He pulls me closer and then He hugs me, even though I am covered with vile muck. But it only seems to make Him love me more! He never once looks away from me and never once has anything but love and grace on His face.

I am totally exhausted and still seem to be unaware that I am now in the loving arms of Jesus, safe and rescued. As the picture ends, the Lord very gently said, "I am there for you always, whether or not you can see Me, or hear Me, or feel Me, or even if you still believe some of satan's lies about Me."

THE SECOND VISION:

My Glorious Present Reality: Restored and
Peaceful in Abba's Loving Arms

A couple of weeks after the dark, horror–filled picture, God graciously gave me another picture of utter love and peace.

In this picture, I find myself looking at a scene so completely blindingly white that at first I cannot make out anything at all. Even though I can at first see nothing but brightness, there is an overwhelming sense of rightness, peace, wholeness, calm, and rest.

As my eyes adjust to this wonderful brightness, I begin to see what looks like the back of a large figure dressed all in white—and all the brightness and whiteness seem to come from Him. I see that this large figure has white hair and white clothes, and He seems to be sitting on an elaborate white throne. I quickly realize that I am coming up behind God the Father on His throne in Heaven.

As I get closer, I am able to look over His shoulder. As my eyes adjust more and more to His beautiful brightness, I see that God is holding something fairly small in His huge arms. Whatever it is, is dressed in brightness just like God is. Then to my complete surprise, I see that it is me, fully-grown me, but held by God, just like a little baby cradled in His arms, fast asleep! There is an overwhelming sense of peace, contentment, love, care, and safety and a pure rest of spirit, soul, and body.

As I watch and marvel at this incredible and spectacular sight, I start to become aware that God and I are not alone in some side room, but we're in the throne room of Heaven. I start to hear voices of all kinds getting louder and louder with praises and worship for my great Abba (Papa) Father. I start to get embarrassed, knowing that all of Heaven is worshipping God, but I am sleeping. As I watch, I see fully-grown "baby" me start to wake up and realize that he has been sleeping while all of Heaven worships Abba Father. This sleepy little baby starts to struggle to sit up and join in with the rest of the worshipping voices.

But Abba Father bends down close to my face and ever so gently says, "Shhh. It's okay. You don't need to join in just now. Rest, My dear child. It's okay. I know your heart. Just rest here in My arms!"

As I watch this beautiful, amazing scene, I am overwhelmed even more, totally undone and completely melted by Abba's immeasurable love, care, and enjoyment of me in His arms, just sleeping—not doing anything!

A great freeing and liberating sense came over me as I realized that I would never have to perform, impress, or strive to get Abba to love me. There is no need to be somebody or do anything; all I need to do is be myself in His great, loving arms. God, the Creator of the entire universe, loves to spend time

with me, even if all I do is rest trustingly in His arms!
Oh, the joy of His great love!
Thank You, Abba!
Thank You from the depths of my heart!

LET'S ASK HIM:

> Jesus, my precious Savior, give me the child-like faith to believe that I am forever in Your great, loving arms—even if sometimes I may fail You.
>
> Abba, my precious Father, give me the child-like trust to believe that I don't have to earn, deserve, or strive to be completely loved and accepted by You.
>
> Fill me to overflowing with Your powerful Spirit, and empower me to love, adore, and live for You, far beyond my own human abilities—for Your glory!
>
> I love You with all my heart, because You have first loved me with all Your Heart.
>
> Thank You for Your great, eternal, astounding Father–Love. It is far, far beyond measure!

For further details and information on ordering more copies, please visit: www.astoundingfatherlove.com.